EVERY PERSON'S GUIDE TO PSALMS

BY RON ISAACS

Published by
The L'Chayim Library
An imprint of Higher Ground Books & Media
Springfield, Ohio
www.highergroundbooksandmedia.com

Printed in the United States of America 2026

Cover Illustration by: Irwin Davis

EVERY PERSON'S GUIDE TO PSALMS

BY RON ISAACS

DEDICATION

Let every breath be praise of God, halleluyah (Psalm 150)

Contents

Introduction

Over one sixth of the Bible is written in poetic form, and about one-half of that has been sung. The Book of Psalms is a collection of poems which have been on the lips of more people throughout the centuries than any other written compositions. They represent the highest product of the religious poetry of all the nations and stand out unique among the prayers of the whole world by the majesty of their language and their simplicity.

Name and Description

The English name Psalms is derived from the Latin Vulgate *Liber Psalmorum*. The Latin, in turn, was borrowed from the *Septuagint*, the Greek version of the Bible, where it was used in the sense of a song accompanied by the playing of a stringed instrument. It thus seems to be a translation of the Hebrew term *mizmor* ("song") which occurs 57 times in the individual captions to the various Psalms.

In rabbinic literature, the designation of the Book of Psalms is "Sefer Tehillim"--"the Book of Praises. (*Talmud, Baba Batra 14b*), sometimes contracted to *Tillim*" (*Talmud Avodah Zarah 19a*). The name *Sefer Tehillim* has passed into traditional usage among the Jewish people, although only one Psalm in the Book of Psalms (*Psalm 145*) has the word *tehillah* in its superscription.

When referring to Psalms included in the Jewish liturgy, the rabbinic authorities mention them as "verses of praise" employing the Aramaic term *zimra*, which is cognate with the Hebrew *mizmor*. The root meaning is to play instrumental music, and then to sing to accompaniment, which in effect explains the origin of most of the compositions in the Book of Psalms. The singing of hymns by a Levitical choir and by the assembly of worshippers, with an accompaniment of string and wind instruments, was a basic feature of the Temple worship service.

Place in the Canon

In the printed Hebrew Bible, the Book of Psalms is the first of the Writings. However, it did not always occupy this position, having formerly been preceded by the Book of Ruth. (Talmud Baba Batra 14b). According to another arrangement, formerly in vogue among the Sephardic Jews, Chronicles preceded the Book of Psalms. The Church Father of the fourth through the fifth century Jerome, assigned the first place to Job followed by Psalms.

Clearly the importance of the Book of Psalms is attested to by the fact that despite the great variety in the order of the Books of the so-called Writings, Psalms either heads the list or is very close to the top of it.

Number of Psalms and Divisions into Books

In the enumeration of the Masoretic text there are a total of 150 Psalms. The *Jerusalem Talmud*, however, has an allusion to 147, the number being obtained by combining 1 and 2, 9 and 10, 114 and 115. *The Encyclopedia Judaica*, (Volume 13, pg. 1306) presents evidence for the existence of widely varying traditions regarding the number of Psalms in the Book of Psalms. For instance, a Psalter of 147 chapters is mentioned in the *Jerusalem Talmud Shabbat 16:1.* The *Leningrad Codex B Bible* features a division into 149 Psalms. Other traditions comprise divisions of from 148 to as many as 170 psalms.

The *Midrash* on Psalms remarks that 'Moses gave Israel the Five Books of the Torah, and correspondingly David gave them the Five Books of the Psalms.

Each of the first four books are marked off by a doxology, or formulaic expression of praise to God as follows:

Book I, Psalms 1-41

41:14 Blessed is the Lord, God of Israel,
From eternity to eternity.

Amen and Amen.

Book II, Psalms 42-72
72: 18-20 Blessed is the Lord God, God of Israel,
Who alone does wondrous things.
Blessed be God's glorious name forever.
And let God's glory fill the whole world.
Amen and Amen. End of the Prayers of David
son of Jesse.

Book III, Psalms 73-89
89:53 Blessed be the Lord to eternity.
Amen and amen.

Book IV, Psalms 90-106
106:48 Blessed is the Lord, God of Israel,
From eternity to eternity.
And let all the people say Amen. Halleluyah.

Book V, Psalms 107-150. (The last book bears no closing formula)

Commentators have asserted that the liturgical character of the psalm doxologies would seem to prove that the book divisions were originally fixed for purposes of public worship, and that it can hardly be accidental that the Book of Psalms opens with a reference to the study of Torah.

Authorship

Of the 150 psalms, 100 are ascribed, in their superscriptions, to various authors by name; one, Psalm 90, is ascribed to Moses; seventy-three Psalms are ascribed to David; Psalms 72 and 177 to Solomon; twelve Psalms (Psalm 50 and Psalms 73-83) to Asaph; Psalm 85 to Heman; Psalm 89 to Ethan; ten to the sons of Korach. In the Septuagint ten more psalms are credited to David.

Although Jewish tradition ascribes the Book of Psalms to King David, nowhere in the entire Bible is there any indication of Davidic authorship of the Book of Psalms. As mentioned earlier, although seventy-three of the 150 psalms are designated *le-David* (concerning David), the precise connotation of this terms is uncertain. The term could mean that the Psalm was connected in content with an event in King David's life, or a tune or style supposedly Davidic in origin, or a composition taken from the repertoire of a Davidic guild of singers.

The first explicit claim to the Davidic origin of the entire Book of Psalms is found in rabbinic literature (*Talmud, Baba Batra 15a*) which draws a comparison between the five books of Davidic psalms and the Five Book of Moses. There can be no doubt that the association of David with Psalm composition rests on David's reputation as a skillful player on the lyre in his earlier youth. *(I Samuel 16:16-23*) and as a "sweet singer of Israel" *(II Samuel 23:1)*

Thus, there is certainly a good probability that David inaugurated a new style of Hebrew lyrical poetry, the Psalm, and was responsible for at least some of the compositions of the Book of Psalms. Critical scholarship of the 19th century regarded the Psalms as the product of the Maccabean-Hasmonean era. This view was grounded in the conviction of the late development of pure monotheism in Israel with its concomitant that the Psalms postdated the prophets. Twentieth century scholarship has generally asserted far greater antiquity of the biblical Psalms.

As to who was responsible for the final selection of the Psalms that finally entered into the Book of Psalms as we know it today, some commentators have asserted that the work of editing was likely done in the time of the Scribes who succeeded Ezra and Nehemiah. Others have assigned the final compilation of the Book of Psalms to the first third of the century immediately preceding the Christian era.

Types of Psalms

There are many ways of classifying the Psalms, and any attempt to systematize them has generally been more an exercise in convenience than precision.

Dr. A. Cohen, in his commentary on the *Book of Psalms* (*Soncino Press, 1962*) offers the following three main typologies:

1. Praise: Most common of all is the extolling of God for His goodness and mercy to Israel and all His creations, His vindication of the righteous when persecuted by the wicked, His kingship of mankind, and His might as Creator and Ruler of the world. Allied themes are praise of the Torah which contains God's revealed will, of Zion chosen by God as His dwelling place on earth, and of David and his dynasty appointed by God to sit on the throne of Israel.

2. Elegy: The minor key is struck in numerous Psalms which tell of the sufferings of individuals and of Israel as a people. In agreement with the accepted doctrine that personal and national calamity is the sequel of sin, earnest confession of guilt and the plea for pardon appear conspicuously in this group.

3. Ethics: Several Psalms are instructive or didactic in nature. They treat of the right way of living, denounce prevalent vices which bring unhappiness to the people, and proclaim the joy which ensues from loyalty to God's will.

According to Professor Nachum Sarna, the leading genre of the Book of Psalms is the hymn, a poem of praise celebrating the majesty and providence of God. Examples of such Psalms include Psalms 8, 29,33,65,66,92,100,104,113,114,117,135 and 145-150. Several Psalms, called "enthronement Psalms", specifically extol God's royal role in the universe and so are often regarded as forming a special category within the hymn. Examples of this type of Psalm are: 47,93,96-99. Another group (Psalm 46,48,76,84,87 and 122) glorifies God's city, God's holy mount in which God has placed His dwelling. These are designated as Zion Songs.

About one third of the Book of Psalms is given over to laments in which the speaker may be either the individual or the community. The latter type bewails situations of national oppression or misfortune (e.g., Psalm 44,60,74,79,80,83,94). The former comprises about forty Psalms in all and is distinguished according to Sarna by personal complaints of bodily or mental suffering which are often accompanied by protestations of innocence and are usually coupled with a strong plea for divine help. Such Psalms include: 3,5,6,7,9-10,13, 17,22,25-28,31,35,36,38,39,41,42-43,51,52,54-57,59,61,63,64,69,71,77,86,88,102,120,123,130,140-143.

A distinctive feature of many of the laments is the expression by the worshipper of the certainty that his prayers will be heard. These so-called "psalms of confidence" may be both collective (e.g., Psalm 46,125,129) or individual in nature, the latter being more frequent. (e.g., Psalm 4,11,16,23,27,62,91,121).

Closely related to the hymn and lament are the thanksgiving psalms. Here again, community songs are relatively rare (e.g., Psalm 66, 67,118,136). This may be since many of the hymns may have had their origin in a national song of thanksgiving. The Psalms in which the speaker is an individual are Psalms 9-10,18,30,34,40,111 and 138.

A class in itself are the "royal psalms" in which the center of attention is the anointed one of God, the earthly king of Israel. His relationship to God, his ideal qualities, the misfortunes that befall him, and the woes that afflict him may all be the themes of the song. (Psalm 2,18,20,21,45,72,89,110,132,144,61,63,84). Sarna also adds Psalms 44 and 101, even though they contain no direct reference to the reigning monarch, but which appear to have been liturgies recited by him, probably belonging within this same category.

Sarna identifies one final major category, provided by those compositions which betray the influence of wisdom literature, or which have a distinctly pedagogic function or character. They may be reflective or sententious (Psalm 1, 34, 36, 37, 49, 73, 78, 112, 127, 128, 133) or descriptive of the kind of conduct pleasing to God

(Psalm 15,24,32,40,50). They also may be an historical retrospect which either directly or inferentially project the lessons to be derived from the past and which are deemed to be relevant to the occasion of the psalm. (Psalm 78,81,105,106,114)

Psalms in Rabbinic Thought

The rabbis reduced the traditional numbers of psalms to 147 according to the *Midrash* on Psalms 22:19. They did this for homiletical purposes as is evident from the passage in the tractate of *Berachot 9b-10a.* In this passage the rabbis explain that Psalm 19:15 was instituted to be recited after the eighteen blessings of the Amidah since it comes at the end of Psalm 18. Whereupon the rabbis ask: "But this is the 19th Psalm, not the 18th, and answer that Psalms 1 and 2 constitute one psalm. It brings evidence for this in the statement that David first uses the word *Halleluyah* at the end of the 103rd Psalm, where in fact it is in Psalm 104:35. Thus it seems quite apparent that at that time Psalms 1 and 2 normally constituted two psalms, and Psalms 19 and 104 were numbered as they are today.

According to Nachum Sarna, the homiletical purpose of the reduction of psalms to 147 is reflected in the statement "Moses gave the five books of the Torah to Israel, and corresponding to them, David gave the five books of the Psalms to Israel. (*Midrash, Psalms 1:2*). To emphasize this relationship, the number of psalms was reduced to 147, to make it correspond to the number of sedarim (ordered portions) in the Bible according to the triennial cycle in current Israel.

Following is a cross section of other rabbinic comments and quotations related to the Book of Psalms, as culled from both Talmudic and midrashic sources:

1. The Book of Psalms includes the compositions of ten earlier authorities: Adam, Melchizedek, Abraham, Moses, Heman, Jeduthun, Asaph, and the three sons of Korach. (*Talmud Baba Batra*

14b, 15a)

2. The Book of Psalms was called after David because "his voice was pleasant." *(Song of Songs Rabbah 4:4, no 1*, referring to *II Samuel 23:1).*

3. All the psalms were inspired (*Talmud Pesachim 117a)* and music helped to bring the inspiration: "A harp was suspended above the bed of David. When midnight came the north wind blew on it and it produced music of its own accord. Immediately David arose and occupied himself with Torah." That "Torah" consisted of songs and praises, however, since "until midnight he occupied himself with Torah. And from then on with songs and praises. (*Talmud Berachot 3b)*

4. The rabbis singled out Psalms 113-118 as the Hallel psalms, the only ones which formed part of the liturgy back in Talmudic times. According to the *Talmud Berachot 56a,* these psalms were known as the "Egyptian Hallel" (*Talmud Berachot 56a*), to distinguish it from Psalms 145-150 and Psalm 136, which are also variously referred to as *Hallel. (Talmud Shabbat 118b*) or Psalm 136 as *Hallel ha-Gadol. (Talmud Pesachim 118a)*

5. The rabbis designated seven psalms which were "the psalms which the Levites used to recite in the Temple" (Tamid 7:4). These have been included in the liturgy today and are recited each day as the Psalm of the Day. They are Psalm 24 (Sunday), Psalm 48 (Monday), Psalm 82 (Tuesday), Psalm 94 (Wednesday), {Psalm 81 (Thursday), Psalm 93 (Friday) and Psalm 92 (Saturday).

6. According to the rabbis, such great importance was attached to Psalm 145 that it was said that "one who recites it three times a day is certain to be granted a place in the world to come." (*Talmud Berachot 4b)*

7. Psalm 16 compresses into eleven principles the whole of the Torah. *(Makkot 24a)*

8. Fifteen of the Psalms are known as Songs of Degrees or Ascent. (120-134) The *Mishnah* of *Sukkot 5:4* and *Middot 2:5* finds a connection with the fifteen steps joining the court of the Israelites to the court of women in the Second Temple on which the Levitical musicians used to stand during the ceremony of the "drawing of water" on Sukkot.

9. The Book of Psalms is regarded as a second Five Books of Moses, whose virtual composer was David, often likened to Moses. *(Midrash Psalms, chapter 1*)

10. According to the great sage Rav, the proper designation of the Book of Psalms would be *Halleluyah*, because the term comprehends both the Divine Name and its glorification, and for this reason is held to be the best of the ten words for praise occurring in the Psalms. These ten words, corresponding in number to the ten men who had a part in composing Psalms, are *beracha* (blessing), *hallel* (praise), *tefillah* (prayer), *shir* (song), *mizmor* (psalm), *neginah (*melody), *natzeach* (to play on an instrument), *ashrei* (happy), *hodot* (thanks) and *halleluyah.* (praise be God). (*Midrash Psalms)*

11. The Hebrew word *ashrei* is found twenty-two times in the Book of Psalms, corresponding to the twenty-two letters of the Hebrew alphabet. (*Midrash, Psalms 37)*

12. Psalms were sung by the Levites immediately after the daily libation of wine. Every liturgical Psalm was sung in three parts. (*Talmud Sukkah 4:5)* During the intervals between the parts the sons of Aaron blew three different blasts on the trumpet. (*Talmud Tamid 7:3)*

13. Psalms 30, the Psalm for the dedication of the Temple was reserved for recitation on Hanukkah. *(Soferim 18:2)*

Superscriptions and Technical Terms in the Book of Psalms

1. **Orphan Psalms**: Only 24 Psalms have no headings of any sort. They are Psalms 1,2,10,33,43,71,93-97,99,104,105,107,114-119,136, and 137.

2. ***Tehillim leDavid*:** Psalms that relate to the name of David. They are distributed as follows:
Book I, 37 (3-9,11-32,34-41).
Book II, 18 (51-65,68-70).
Book III, one (86)
Book IV, two (101,103)
Book V, 15 (108-110,122,123, 131,133,138,145)

3. **Psalms of Asaph:** Two Psalms are associated with Asaph (50, 73-83).

4. **Psalms of the Korahites**: There are eleven Korahite psalms (42,44-49,84-85,87-88. The Korahites are first recorded as participating in the Temple worship service at the time of King Jehoshaphat (II Chronicles 20:19).

5. **Psalms of Heman and Ethan**: Only one psalm each is assigned to Heman and Ethan. (Psalm 88,89) Both are entitled "Ezrahite." They were both leaders of the Temple musicians under David.

6. **Psalm of Moses:** Psalm 90 is attributed to Moses. According to Bible commentators, this is likely based on the affinities between verse 1 (O God, You have been our refuge in every generation) and *Deuteronomy 33:27 (*The ancient God is a refuge) and verse 10 (The span of our life is seventy years, or given the strength, eighty years) and *Exodus 7:7* (Moses was eighty years old and Aaron eighty three

when they made their demand on Pharaoh).

Title with Liturgical Application

1. Psalm 30: Dedication of the Temple: The heading of Psalm 30 mentions the dedication of the Temple, which must be a reference to the occasion of its recitation.

2. **Psalm 100: *Mizmor Letodah*:** A psalm of thanksgiving, implying a liturgy for the sacrificial todah offering.

3. **Psalm 92**: This Psalm has as its heading a Psalm for the Sabbath Day.

Modern Ritualistic Uses of Psalms

For hundreds of years both the Jewish people and others too, have turned to the Book of Psalms for comfort, consolation, guidance, renewal, and much more. Indeed, the 150 Psalms reflect a wide range of experience and expression--anger and acceptance, grievance and comfort, despair and faith. Psalms also pervade the liturgy of morning, afternoon and evening prayers, and there is a Psalm of the Day which allows the worshipper a chance to reflect and meditate on the words that the ancient Levites themselves sang when acting as the choir in the ancient Temple.

Rabbi Simkha Y. Weintraub, the Rabbinic Director of the National Center for Jewish Healing ("*From the Depths: Psalms as a Spiritual Reservoir in Difficult Times", National Center for Jewish Healing Newsletter, Volume 2, Issue 2, Fall 1999)* identifies the following seven functions that Psalms have developed in Jewish life:

Ritual: As a source of regular expression, to mark certain moments and create a container for feelings, ideas, and values, either in an established traditional, communal context or in one's own personal, innovative time and place. He cites one example of a Jewish support group that began each meeting with a Psalm of despair or complaint (such as 13, 77 or 88) and ended with a Psalm of gratitude. (such as 18,91 or 118)

Prayer: As with other forms of Jewish prayer, Psalms may provide various opportunities for giving words to hopes, fears and wishes.

Song: So many lines of Psalms have been put to music, and even calling on the melodies without the words can have great impact. Weintraub cites examples of lines from Psalms that have become known as "Jewish healing Songs" because of their words and/or music: *Psalm 27:4* ("One thing I ask of God"); *Psalm 118:5* ("From the Narrow Straits); *Psalm 121:1-2* ("I will lift up my eyes")

Study: the Hebrew of the Psalms is often obscure or otherwise hard to "crack," having gone through centuries of recopying. This means that there is a lot to explore.

Meditation: Words of Psalms can be a valuable tool in refocusing, centering, and quieting oneself. Weintraub notes that some people post a verse, phrase or word on their office computer screen so they can freely turn to it during a workday; others make their own audio recording to be able to play it back while sitting in a quiet, undisturbed setting.

Community: There are "Psalm Fellowship" groups today, which gather regularly to study or chant Psalms together. In some communities when a person is ill, the 150 Psalms have been predivided by members so that the entire *Book of Psalms* is read and dedicated daily to healing, solace and recovery.

Conversation: Weintraub also recommends weaving important words and phrases in Psalms into one's own vocabulary and speech.

Technical Terms in Psalm Headings

1. ***Mizmor***: Appears in 57 of the book of Psalms, it is generally translated as Psalm (deriving from the translation "psalmos") in the Septuagint. Mizmor refers to liturgical music.

2. ***Lamenatzeach*:** Occurs in 55 psalms, and it also believed to refer to liturgical performance.

3. ***Shir***: Appears in 30 psalms and is generally translated as song.

4. ***Shir ha-Maalote*:** Appears at the head of a cluster of psalms 120-134. Rabbinic thought understands the Hebrew word "maalote" to mean steps and finds a connection with the fifteen steps joining the court of the Israelites to the court of women in the Second Temple on which the Levitical musicians used to stand during the ceremony of the drawing of water. Other commentators posit a connection of the psalms of ascent with the return from Babylon.

5. ***Maskil***: Featured in the headings to 13 psalms, it has been assumed to refer to a special skill *required in the manner of a musical performance.*

6. ***Michtam****:* Appears in six psalms. In the *Septuagint michtam* is translated as an inscription upon a slab. Others connect the word with an Akkadian root meaning "to cover" and assume a connection with some atonement rite.

7. ***Tefillah*:** Appearing in the superscriptions to five psalms. *Tefillah* is translated as prayer.

8. ***Al Shoshannim*, *Al Shushan Edut* and *El Shoshannim Edut*:** *Al shoshanim* may be translated "on the lilies" *(Psalm 45:69*), *El shushan edut* may be translated "on the lily of testimony" (*Psalm 60*) and *shoshannim edut* may be translated "to the lilies of testimony."

(*Psalm 80)* Nachum Sarna posits that they may be cue words (i.e., the titles of some well-known songs to the turn of which the psalm was sung.) The reference may also be to a six-stringed instrument shaped like a lily.

9. ***Al Tashchet*:** Found in headings of Psalms 57-59, the Hebrew means "do not destroy." It has been conjectured that it may be the name of a song of which perhaps a remnant is found in *Isaiah 65:8* "...One says, do not destroy, there is good in it."

10. ***Al Machalat***: The word "machalat" literally means sickness. Perhaps it is an abbreviation of the Hebrew *machalat Leannot* ("sickness to afflict") in Psalm 88--the name of a melody, evidently in a minor key, to which the Psalm was chanted.

11. ***Al Alamot*:** Found only in the heading of Psalm 46, the word means "maidens". It is conjectured that it refers to a musical instrument with a high pitch.

12. ***Al Mut Laben*:** Appearing only in Psalm 9, it literally means "death to the son." The ancient Jewish commentators explained that David composed this poem on the death of a neighboring ruler, named Labben, who has oppressed Israel. However, there is no record of such a person in the Bible. By analogy it is most likely a direction to the leader of the orchestra, indicating the name of a song whose melody was to accompany the psalm.

12. ***Al ayelet Hashachar*:** Literally meaning "the hind of the morning", in all probability it was the name of the melody to the accompaniment of which the Psalm was to be rendered. It only appears in Psalm 22.

13. ***Al Yonat Elem Rechokim*:** Appearing only in Psalm 56, the meaning is "the silent dove of them that are distant." It is conjectured that it is most likely the title of a song to whose melody the Psalm

was sung.

14. ***Shigayyon***: Appearing in Psalm 7, it has often been understood as meaning a psalm of lamentation.

Psalms in the Liturgy

The introduction of various psalms was a gradual process that took place over the centuries. During Talmudic times the statutory prayers included no psalms whatsoever on Sabbaths and weekdays. The only psalms recited were the so-called *Hallel Psalms* (113-118) on the three Pilgrim Festivals (*Sukkot, Passover* and *Shavuot*) as well as on *Hanukkah*. Later the *Hallel* service was also added to *Rosh Hodesh,* the New Moon Festival occurring each month at the beginning of the month

Statutory Prayers

The Book of Psalms may be said to the hymn book of the people of Israel during the existence of the Second Temple. The hymns were sung either by the Levites in the Temple or by the people. According to Talmudic tradition, psalms were sung by the Levites immediately after the daily libation of wine. And every liturgical Psalm was sung in three parts. (*Talmud Sukkah 4:5)* During the intervals between the parts the sons of Aaron blew three different blasts on the trumpet. (*Tamid 7:3)*

The process whereby the recitation of psalms became a central component of the statutory prayers consisted of regarding each reference to the recitation of Psalms in the Talmud either as acts of special piety performed by individuals, or part of the Temple service, as a justification for making them part of the statutory service. To this class belong the *Pesukei de-Zimra* (Songs of Praise) and the Daily Psalm, or Psalm of the Day. The *Pesukei de-Zimra,,* chanted at the beginning of the worship, originally consisted of the six last Psalms of the *Book of Psalms*, namely Psalms 145-150. Their recitation is mentioned in the *Talmud Shabbat 118b),* whereas in the post-Talmudic tractate of Soferim they are simply called the "six daily Psalms" which are already part of the statutory service. (*Talmud Soferim 17:11)*

On the principle that there was more leisure time on Sabbaths and festivals, both the Ashkenazi and Sephardi rites add a considerable number of Psalms on those days: the Ashkenazi rite adds nine Psalms (19,34,90,91,135,136,33,92 and 93). The Sephardic rite adds fourteen Psalms (103,19,33,90,91,98,121,124,135,136,92,93) A similar process is seen regarding the Daily Psalms. They are mentioned in the *Midrash (Tam. 7:4)* as "the psalms which the Levites used to sing in the Temple." By the time of the Soferim they are already part of the daily prayers, "the people having adopted the custom. (18:1) However, here again, once the transfer was made to the synagogue, it was extended to special psalms for every festival. In the course of time many individual psalms were added: Psalm 30 before the *Pesukei de-Zimra*, Psalm 100 on weekdays in the *Pesukei de-Zimra,* Psalm 6 in the supplicatory prayers, Psalm 24 on weekdays when the Torah scroll is returned to the Ark, and Psalm 29 on Sabbaths and festivals. Psalm 20 was included in the last portion of the daily service. Psalm 27 was instituted for the penitential period from the second day of *Elul* to *Hoshanah Rabbah*, while Psalms 144 and 67 were instituted for the Service that bids farewell to the holy Sabbath.

Psalms 104 and the so-called *Fifteen Songs of Ascent*, included in the Sabbath afternoon *Mincha* service during the winter months, were instituted in the 12th century. In the 16th century Psalms 95-99 and Psalm 20 were instituted by the Kabbalists as part of the *Kabbalat Shabbat* service on Friday evening.

In modern times, the psalms continue to permeate the prayerbooks of the various branches of Judaism. The authorized Daily Prayer Book of the United Hebrew Congregation of England (Singer) gives an index of 73 psalms in the various services. In the *Sim Shalom* prayerbook of the Conservative Movement there is an index of 58 psalms.

Non-Statutory Prayers

There is no special or non-statutory service which does not include one or more psalms. They include the introduction to the grace after meals, prayers for drought, before going on a journey, the night prayer before going to sleep, prayers for and by the sick, the burial service, the prayer in the house of mourning, the *Yizkor* memorial service for the dead, and the service called the unveiling for the consecration of a tombstone. Under the influence of mystics, a special custom has developed regarding Psalm 119, the eightfold alphabetic Psalm. At memorial services verses are chosen which make up the name of the deceased and his parents.

Other Customs

The regular reading of Psalms is not only confined to services. In recent years there are Psalm societies that have been created, where people as a group recite the entire Book of Psalms over an agreed upon period of time and in a prescribed order. Some families today have the custom of reciting a different psalm before beginning the Friday evening festival Sabbath meal.

The One Hundred and Fifty Psalms

Following is an outline and summary of each of the 150 Psalms in the Book of Psalms. Each Psalm will be described using the following paradigm:

Theme: The main point of the Psalm
Outline of Psalm: An outline of the structure of the Psalm
Liturgical Use: How the Psalm is used liturgically. (i.e., where and when it is used in the worship service)
Practical Use: Suggestions as to when the Psalm might be used in a real- life situation.
Legends: Midrashic legendary texts related to the Psalm.
Notable Quotations: Noteworthy verses in the Psalm.

Psalm 1

Theme: The contrast and fate of the godly person and ungodly person is the subject matter of this wisdom Psalm. The godly person derives strength of purpose from God, while the wicked will receive chastisement at God's hands. The psalm serves as an excellent precis to the entire Book of Psalms.

Outline: 1-3 The way of the godly. Happiness awaits the good.
4-6 The way of the ungodly. The netherworld awaits the impious.

Liturgical Use: Part I of the Psalm is often used at a funeral of consecration of a tombstone.

Practical Use: i. When studying Torah or having doubts about faith.
ii. Confused by success of wicked, envious of the rich.
iii. Doubts about faith.

Legends: This legend questions the literal meaning of the psalm, and addresses the question related to the opening verse in *Psalm 1*: If a blessed man is one who does not walk in the way of the wicked, how could such a man be described in the next part of the verse as standing in the way of sinners.

Blessed is the man that walks not in the counsel of the wicked, nor stands in the way if sinners, nor sits in the seat of the scornful" *(Psalm 1:1)*. Rabbi Simeon be Pazzi commented: If he walks not, how could he be standing on the way? And if he stands not on the way, how could he come to sit in the seat of the scornful? And if he sits not among them, how could he scoff with them? The verse means to tell you, however, that when a man walks among the wicked, he ends up standing with them; when he stands among them, he ends up sitting with them; and when he sits among them, he ends up by scoffing with them. And when he scoffs, it is of him that Scripture says, "If you scorn, you alone shall bear it" *(Proverbs 9:12) [Talmud Avodah Zarah 18b)*

Notable Quotations:

1. He shall be like a stream planted by streams of water,
That brings forth its fruit in its season,
And whose leaf does not wither.
And in whatsoever he does he shall prosper. (1:3)

2. Not so the wicked.
But they are like the chaff which the wind drives away. (1:4)

Psalm 2

Theme: The theme of the Psalm is an exemplification of the proverb, 'Man proposes, God disposes.' Clearly this is a royal psalm, composed for a coronation. Commentators differ as to whether the subject of the Psalm is the messianic or historical king, and if the latter, who he was. It is often understood as pre-exilic, coming from a time when the nation was surrounded by powerful foes and national feeling running high.

Outline: 1-3 The rebellion of local kings against the new overlord
4-6 God speaks to the plotting nations and derides the plot and their behavior
7-9 The king speaks and tells of a divine oracle that he has received.
10-12 The psalmist appeals to the plotting kings explaining the reconciliation to be effected. Punishment awaits the intractable, reward the obedient.

Liturgical Use: None

Practical Use: When having doubts about faith.

Legends: This legend attempts to demonstrate, using a verse in *Psalm 2*, that one should only rise for the Amidah prayer in a reverent frame of mind.

One should not stand up to say the Tefillah except in a reverent frame of mind. The pious men of yore used to spend an hour in meditation and pray only after that, to make sure that their hearts would be directed to their Father in heaven.

And the proof from the Bible? From the verse "worship God in the beauty (hadrat) of holiness" *(Psalm 29:2),* concerning which

Rabbi Joshua ben Levi said, Read not *hadrat*,, but *herdat*, "awe." But Rabbi Nachman bar Isaac said, from another verse: "Serve the Lord with fear and rejoice with trembling" *(Psalm 2:11)*, which according to Rav, means: Where there is rejoicing, there is also to be trembling. (*Talmud Berachot 30b)*

Notable Quotations

1. He that sits in heavens laughs,
God has them in derision. (2:1)

2. Serve the Lord with fear,
And rejoice with trembling. (2:11)

3. Happy are they that take refuge in God. (2:12)

Psalm 3

Theme: This psalm is a personal lament in which the psalmist prays for deliverance from his enemies. It is a sublime expression of trust in God's help when beset by relentless enemies.

Outline:

1-2	The psalmist's perilous position.
3-5	God is a shield of protection
6-7	No need to be afraid
8-9	Prayer for deliverance

Liturgical Use: Not appearing in prayerbook

Practical Use: Anxiety from enemies and all occasions when one is in a perilous situation.

Legends: This legend attempts to explain the meaning of the word "psalm" in the opening verse of *Psalm 3* "A psalm of David when he fled from his son Absalom."

"A psalm of David when he fled from his son Absalom" *(Psalm 3:1)* "A psalm of David?" Scripture should have said, "A lamentation of David." Rabbi Simeon ben Avishalom explained David's use of "psalm" by the parable of a man against whom a writ of debt is issued. Before he pays is, he is troubled. After he has paid it, he is glad. So it is with David. When the Holy One said to him, "Behold, I will raise up evil against you out of your own house" (II *Samuel 12:11*), he was troubled, saying to himself: Perhaps it will be a slave or a bastard who will have no pity on me. But when he saw that it was Absalom, he was relieved, saying: A son is likely to have pity on his father. (*Talmud Berachot 7b)*

Notable Quotations:

1. Many there are that say of my soul,'
   There is salvation for him in God.' Selah. (3:1)

2. I am not afraid of ten thousands of people,
   That have set themselves against me round about. (3:7)

3. Salvation belongs to God.
   Your blessing be upon your people. (3:9)

Psalm 4

Theme: The Jewish community has fallen upon difficult times, and a drought has overtaken the land. The psalmist is very distressed while the leaders of the people criticize God and seek rain from the nature deities. The psalmist reminds the people that God will listen to their prayer if they show contrition for their transgressions and offer proper sacrifices.

Outline: 1-4 Appeal to God and psalmist's enemies
4-6 Appeal to enemy to commune with their hearts and stop transgressing
7-9 Psalmist's trust in God

Liturgical Use: None

Practical Use: i. To be recited when one has difficulty falling asleep.
ii. When feeling threatened, anxious or afraid.

Legends: Using verse 4 of *Psalm 5* (i.e., commune with your own heart upon your bed) as one of its illustrations, this legend attempts to expound upon the meaning of the verse "God is the hope (*mikveh)* of Israel" (*Jeremiah 17: 13)*

Rabbi Eliezer ben Jacob said: "The Lord is the hope (mikveh) of Israel" (*Jeremiah 17:13)* means that as the ritual bath of purification (mikveh) cleanses those who are unclean, so the Holy Blessed One cleanses Israel.

Hence the Holy Blessed One declared to Israel: When you pray, pray in the synagogue in your city; if you cannot pray in the synagogue in your city, pray in your open field; if you cannot pray in your open field, pray in your house; if you cannot pray in your house, pray on your bed; if you cannot pray aloud in your bed, commune with your heart. Hence it is written, "Commune with your own heart upon your bed, and be still. Selah" *(Psalm 4:5) (Midrash Tehillim 4:9)*

Notable Quotations:

1. Answer me when I call, O God of my righteousness, (4:1)

2. You did set me free when I was in distress
   Be gracious to me and hear my prayer. (4:2)

3. Tremble, and do not sin,
   Commune with your own heart upon your bed and be still. Selah. (4:5)

4. In peace will I both lay me down and sleep.
   For You, God, makes me dwell alone in safety. (4:9)

Psalm 5

Theme: This individual lament is like psalm 4, in that the psalmist is exposed to great danger from lurking foes. He offers a morning prayer in which he expresses his conviction that God who hates evil will never allow the wicked to triumph.

Outline: 1-3 A plea for God's attention
4-7 Contrast between the arrogant sinners and the psalmist
8-9 Psalmist's prayer to God
11-13 Joy of the righteous who receive God's blessing.

Liturgical Use: The verse "But as for me, in the abundance of Your lovingkindness will I come into Your house; I will bow toward Your holy temple in the fear of You" appears in the opening prayer Ma Tovu of every morning worship service. The verse is intended to help to psychologically prepare the worshipper for prayer by encouraging and reminding him or her that a feeling of reverential awe is important to the prayer experience.

Practice Use: i. In the synagogue at the beginning of the prayer service.
ii. Anxiety from enemies.

Legends: This tale attempts to prove that God is a God who does not wish to condemn any creature.

Rabbi Pinchas the Priest bar Hama said: The Holy One does not wish to condemn any creature: "For it is not My desire that anyone shall die, says the Lord God. Repent, therefore, and live" [*Ezekiel 18:32];* "You are not a God who desires to declare guilt" *[Psalm 5:5];* and "As I live, says God--it is not My desire that the wicked shall die" [*Ezekiel 33:11].*

What then does God desire? To vindicate His creatures: "God

desires His servant's vindication" [*Isaiah 42:21]*. You can see this for yourself. When creatures sin and provoke God, and God is provoked at them, what does the Holy One do? He goes around and seeks an advocate who will plead for them, and He himself provides for the advocate a line of argument. Thus, in the days of Jeremiah, you find that God said, "Run to and fro through the streets of Jerusalem, and see now, and know, and seek in the broad places thereof, if you can find a man, if there be any that does justly, that seeks truth, and I will pardon her" [*Jeremiah 5:1]*. So too, when the Sodomites sinned, God revealed the matter to Abraham so that he would plead for them, as intimated in the verse "Shall I hide from Abraham..." *[Genesis 18:17]*. Indeed, Abraham at once began to be plead in their behalf: "And Abraham drew near, and said: 'Will You sweep away the innocent with the guilty?'" *(Genesis 18:23)*. *(Tanchuma, Vayera, parag. 8)*

Notable Quotations:

1. O God, in the morning You shall hear my voice.
   In the morning I will order my prayer to You and will look forward. (5:4)

2. You destroy those that speak falsehood.
   God abhors the person of blood and of deceit. (5:7)

3. But as for me, in the abundance of Your lovingkindness will I come into Your house.
   I will bow down toward Your holy temple in fear of You. (5:8)

Psalm 6

Theme: This is a song of lamentation and a prayer for healing said by the writer who needed healing, having suffered from a wasting disease.

Outline: 2-4 Cry of suffering
5-8 Plea for recovery and deliverance
9-11 Psalmists prayer is heard by God and answered

Liturgical Use: Included in the daily morning liturgy among the penitential prayers of the so-called Tachanun service.

Practical Use: i. Anxiety from enemies
ii. Great trouble and distress
iii. In need of physical or spiritual healing.

Legends: This legend explains the verse "O God, rebuke me not in Your anger" (*Psalm 6:2)* by offering a comparison of an angry God with a king who is angry with his son.

"O God, rebuke me not in Your anger" *(Psalm 6:2).* Rabbi Eleazar said: With whom may God in His punishment of Israel be compared? With a king who became angry at his son and at that moment, holding in his hand an unsheathed Indian sword, swore that he would whip it across his son's head. But then the king softened and said: If I whip it across my son's head, his life will be gone, and who will inherit my kingdom. And yet it is impossible for me to revoke my royal word. What did the king do? He put the sword back into its sheath and then whipped it across his son's head, and so his son was spared while his royal word was kept.

Rabbi Hanina taught: God may be compared with a king who became angry at his son and seeing at that moment a large stone before him, wrote that he would heave it at his son. But then the king said: If I throw it at my son, his life will be gone. What did the king do? He ordered that the stone be broken up into small pebbles and that these be thrown, one by one, at his son. And thus the king spared his son and yet kept his royal oath. (*Midrash Tehillim 6:3; Yalkut, Psalms, parag. 633)*

Notable Quotations:

1. Be gracious to me, O God, for I am wasting away,
   Neither chasten me in Your wrath. (6:1)

2. For in death there is no remembrance of You.
   In the nether world who will give You thanks. (6:6)

3. All of my enemies shall be ashamed and afraid.
   They shall turn back, they shall suddenly be ashamed. (6:11)

Psalm 7

Theme: This psalm of lamentation is another prayer for protection under attack by treacherous enemies. The superscription of the Psalm ascribes the Psalm to David, written about Cush a Benjamite. In the Talmud Cush is identified with King Saul.

Outline: 2-3 The danger of the psalmist
4-6 A solemn protest of innocence against enemy accusations
6-9 Prayer for God's intervention and for God's judgment
12-17 Fate of the wicked (i.e., wicked will fall into its own trap)

Liturgical Use: None.

Practical Use: Anxiety from enemies.

Legends: This is a tale about falsehood and vexation which are anthropomorphized. The *midrash* uses the verse "falsehood has brought forth" *[Psalm 7:15*] as a scriptural proof text.

Rabbi Levi taught: When the Holy One said to Noah, "Gather unto you two living creatures of every kind into the ark," all the creatures came and each of them entered the ark with his mate. Falsehood also came and wished to enter, but Noah said, "You cannot enter unless you wed a proper mate." So, Falsehood went looking for a mate and encountered Vexation. Vexation asked, "Where are your coming from?" Falsehood replied, "From Noah. I wanted to enter the ark, but he would not allow me to do so unless I had a proper mate with me. Would you be willing to be my mate?" Vexation asked, "What will you give me?" Falsehood replied, "I pledge you all that I may lay by, you shall take." [Vexation agreed to Falsehood's proposition] and they both entered the ark. After they left the ark, Falsehood went about laying things by, and Vexation took them, one by one. When Falsehood came and inquired "Where are all the things I laid by?" Vexation replied, "Was it not agreed between us that I would take everything you might lay by?" Falsehood had nothing more to say.

"Yea, vexation has become heavy with what Falsehood has brought forth" *[Psalm 7:15]*. As the proverb puts it: What falsehood begets, vexation takes over. *(Midrash Tehillim 7:11; Yalkut Noah, parag. 56)*

Notable Quotations:

1. Let the enemy pursue my soul and overtake it.
   And tread my life down to the earth.
   Yea, let him lay my glory in the dust. Selah. (7:6)

2. My shield is with God,
   Who saves the upright in heart. (7:11)

3. I will give thanks to God according to His righteousness.
   And will sing praise to the name of the Lord Most High. (7:18)

Psalm 8

Theme: This psalm celebrates God's infinite majesty and the dignity and power to which God has raised man. It also describes the paradox of man. From one point of view, man is relatively insignificant in comparison with the greatness of God's works. On the other hand, man is the ruler of the earth and endowed with powers which make him little less than divine.

Outline: 2-3 God's majesty, an exclamation of reverent awe
3-5 Man's physical insignificance
6-9 Man's spiritual pre-eminence

Liturgical Use: Verses 5 and 6 of this psalm: "What is man that You are mindful of him, and the son of man that You think of him? Yet You have made him but little lower than the angels and have crowned him with glory and honor" are used in some prayerbooks as introductory verses to the Yizkor Memorial Service recited on the Day of Atonement, Shemini Atzeret, Passover and Shavuot.

Practical Use: Anxiety from enemies.

Legends: This legend, using various verses in *Psalm 8,* attempts to illustrate the deliberation that God took when creating Adam, the first human being.

Rabbi Huna said in the name of Rabbi Aibu: God created Adam with due deliberation. He first created the means of man's sustenance and only then did He create him. The ministering angels spoke up to the Holy One: "Master of the Universe, "what is man that You are mindful of him?' *[Psalm 8:5]*. This source of trouble--why should he be created?" "if what you hint in your question is to be followed," God replied, "'sheep and oxen, all of them' [*Psalm 8:8*] --why should they have been created? Why should 'the fowl of the air and the fish of the sea' [*Psalm 8:9]* have been created? I am like a king who has a tower full of good things, but no guests. What joy can the tower give the king who filled it?" At that, the ministering angels declared, "Master of the universe, 'Lord, our Lord, how glorious is Your Name in all the earth' *[Psalm 8:10]*. Do what pleases You." (*Genesis Rabbah 8:6*)

Notable Quotations:

1. Out of the mouth of babes and sucklings have You found strength, Because of Your adversaries; that You might still the enemy and the avenger. (8:3)

2. What is man, that You are mindful of him?
   And the son of man, that You take account of him?
   Yet You have made him but little lower than the angels,
   And have crowned him with glory and honor. (8:5-6)

3. O Lord, our God,
   How glorious is Your name in all the earth. (8:10)

Psalm 9

Theme: A trace of an alphabetical acrostic is discernable in this psalm, a song of thanksgiving and a hymn of praise for victory over national enemies.

Outline: 2-3 Praise to God after victory
4-5 God the vindicator
6-9 Complete annihilation of the enemy
10-11 God the Protector
12-13 God the Avenger
14-15 Prayer of the humble
16-17 Retribution overtakes aggressors
18-19 Fate of the wicked (who return to the netherworld)
20-21 Concluding Prayer

Liturgical Use: None

Practical Use: 1. Anxiety from enemies
2. Feeling of thankfulness to God.

Legends: This legend illustrates a tale based on the verse "Make me not the reproach of the base." (*Psalm 9:9*)

"Make me not the reproach of the base" *(Psalm 9:9)*. Rav Hama bar Hanina said: The nations of the earth should have no sickly or broken-down people among them. Why then are there sickly and broken-down people among them? So that they should not taunt Israel and say, "are you not a people made up of those who are sickly and broken down?" Thus, Israel's prayer "make me not the reproach of the base" is fulfilled.

Rabbi Samuel bar Nachman said: None among the nations of the earth should have persons with running sores. Why then are there among them some who have running sores? So that they should not taunt Israel, saying, "Are you not the people of lepers?" Israel's prayer "Make me not the reproach of the base" is thus fulfilled. (*Genesis Rabbah 88:1; Yalkut, Vayeshev, parag. 146)*

Notable Quotations:

1. I will give thanks to God with my whole heart.
   I will tell of all Your marvelous works. (9:2)

2. God is enthroned forever,
   He has established His throne for judgment. (9:8)

3. The wicked shall return to the nether world,
   Even all the nations that forget God. (9:18)

Psalm 10

Theme: Similar in theme to psalm 9, this psalm is a prayer for divine intervention against the wicked. The chief difference between psalms 9 and 10 is the status of those who cause the innocent suffering. In the previous psalm they were the godless nations who were neighbors of Israel. In Psalm 10, they are godly persons within Israel itself who are oppressing their weaker brother and sisters.

Outline: 1-2 Appeal to God for assistance
3-11 Description of the wicked
17-18 God hears prayers and will right the oppressed

Liturgical Use: None

Practical Use: When perplexed by injustice and God's distance.

Legends: This legend presents the tale which Rabbi Judah says is applicable to the verse "Nay, but for Your sake are we killed all the day; we are accounted as sheep for the slaughter" (*Psalm 44:23).*

"Nay, but for Your sake are we killed all the day; we are accounted as sheep for the slaughter" [Psalm 44:23]. Rabbi Judah said: This verse applies to a certain woman and her seven children, specifically Miriam daughter of Tanhum, who together with her seven sons, was taken captive. The seven sons were taken and placed within the innermost of the seven enclosures of a temple for idol worship.

The eldest was brought before the emperor and told, "Bow down to the idol." He replied, "It is written in the Torah, 'I am the Lord your God'" *[Exodus 20:2]* At once he was taken out and put to death. Then the second son was brought to the emperor and told, "Bow down to the idol." He replied, "It is written in the Torah, 'You shall have no other gods before Me'" *[Exodus 20:3].* He was taken out and put to death. Then the third son was brought and told, "Bow down to the idol." He replied, "It is written in the Torah, 'You shall bow down to no other god'" [Exodus 34:14]. He was taken out and put to death. Then the fourth was brought and told, "Bow down to the idol." He replied, "It is written in the Torah, 'He that sacrifices unto the gods shall be utterly destroyed'" *[Exodus 22:19].* He was taken out and put to death. Then the fifth son was brought and told, "Bow down to the idol." He replied, "It is written in the Torah, 'Hear O Israel, the Lord our God, the Lord is One.'" [Deut. 6:4] He was taken out and put to death. The sixth son was brought and told, "Bow down to the idol." He replied, "it is written in the Torah, 'Know therefore this day, and lay it to your heart, that the Lord, He is God in heaven above and upon the earth beneath; there is none else'" *[Deuteronomy 4:39]* He was taken out and put to death. The seventh son, the youngest, was brought and the emperor said to him, "My son, bow down to the idol." He replied, "God forbid." The emperor asked, "Why not?" The lad answered, "Because it is written in our Torah, 'You have avowed the Lord this day to be your God...and the Lord has avowed you this day' *[Deut. 26:17-18)* We have long ago sworn to the Holy One that we will not exchange Him for any other God, and He also has sworn to us that He will not exchange us for any other people." The emperor said, "Your brothers have had in part their fill of years, full of life, and savored that which is sweet; you are but a child, you have not had your fill of years, your fill of life, and yet not savored that which is sweet in the world. Listen to me and bow down before the idol."

He replied, "it is written in our Torah, 'The Lord shall reign forever and ever' *[Exodus 15:18],* and 'The Lord is King forever; the nations will perish out of His land' *[Psalm 10:16*]. You will cease and your kingdom will cease. But the Holy One lives and endures forever."

The emperor said, "Look at your brothers lying dead before you. I will throw my ring to the ground in front of the idol. Bend over just enough to pick up the ring, so that it will be said, 'He obeyed the emperor's command.'" The lad replied, "Alas for you, O emperor. Alas for you, O emperor. If your honor is so important, how much more and more the honor of the Holy One." As he was taken out and put to death, his mother pleaded, "Give me my son, that I may kiss him." They gave him to her. Then she said, "By the life of your head, O emperor, put me to death first, and then put him to death." The emperor replied, "I cannot agree to that, because in Your Torah it is written, 'You shall not kill it and its young both in one day'" *[Lev. 22:28]*. She said, "Wicked one, have you already fulfilled all the other commandments, and this one alone remains for you to fulfill?" At once the emperor ordered the child to be put to death. The mother threw herself upon the boy, and embraced and kissed him, and said, "My son, go to your father Abraham and tell him, 'This is what my mother said: "Do not be proud. You built one altar, but I built seven altars. Yours was only a test, but mine a reality."' Even as she was embracing and kissing her child, they put him to death in her arms.

Then she went up to the roof and jumped to her death. A divine voice proclaimed, "The mother of such children causes rejoicing" *[Psalm 113:9]. (Talmud Gittin 57b; Lamentations Rabbah 1:16, parag. 50; Yalkut, Lamentations, parag. 1029)*

Notable Quotations

1. Why do You stand afar off, O God?
   Why do you hide Yourself in time of trouble? (10:1)

2. Arise, O God, lift up Your hand;
   Forget not the humble. (10:12)

3. God, You have heard the desire of the humble;
   You will direct their heart, You will cause Your ear to attend. (10:17)

Psalm 11

Theme: This is a song of trust and steadfastness. Similar in setting to Psalms 5 and 7, the Psalmist's life is threatened. Friends advise him to seek safety in flight, but he stands firm because of his confidence in God's divine protection.

Outline: 1-3 Friends advise the Psalmist to flee
4-7 Psalmist's confidence in God

Liturgical Use: None.

Practical Use: Uplifted feeling.

Legends: According to *Psalm 11:5*, "God tests the righteous." This *midras*h presents us with the test.

"The Lord tests the righteous" *[Psalm 11:5*) He tested David by means of the sheep and found him a good shepherd, as is said, "God took him because of his separations." It means that David kept some sheep separate from the others. He would first lead out the young lambs and let them feed on the upper part of the herbage, which is tender; then he would lead out the rams and let them feed on the middle part of the herbage, which is neither tender nor tough. Finally, he would lead out the old ewes and let them feed on the stubble of the herbage, which is tough. So the Holy One said: He who knows how to look after sheep, each according to its capacity, is to look after My sheep--Israel. Hence, "from following the ewes that give suck He brought him, to be shepherd over Jacob His people" *[Psalm 78:1] (Midrash Tehillim 78:21); Exodus Rabbah* 2:2; *Yalkut Psalms, parag. 823)*

Notable Quotations

1. For lo, the wicked bend the bow,

They have made ready their arrow upon the string,
That they may shoot in darkness at the upright in heart. (11:2)

2. God is righteous, and God loves righteousness,
The upright shall behold God's face. (11:7)

Psalm 12

Theme: This psalm, often termed one of the "persecution Psalms", is deemed such because the innocent are beset with slanderous enemies who plot their destruction. The sufferer in this psalm prays for deliverance from his personal enemies and is concerned not only with his own troubles but over the general state of degeneracy which prevails.

Outline: 2-5 Psalmist's prayer
6-9 God's answer and the confidence in His answer

Liturgical Use: None.

Practical Use: Anxiety from one's enemies.

Legends: This story is an illustration of the verse in Psalms "They speak falsehood everyone with his neighbor; with smooth lip, and with a double heart do they speak." ***(Psalm 12:3)***

A story about Rabbi Jonathan at a time when lentils were scarce in his town. He had a kinsman in a certain city, and he went down to him and said, "I am looking for lentils. Are there any to be had in the city?" His kinsman replied, "There are." Rabbi Jonathan asked, "At what price?" His kinsman answered, "At such-and-such a price. Anytime that you come here, I shall get them for you."

After a while, Rabbi Jonathan went to the city and to his kinsman's house, inquiring after him. His kinsman's wife said, "He is in the field." Rabbi Jonathan waited for him, but since he did not appear, Rabbi Jonathan asked one of the men of the city, "Are there lentils to be had here?" The man answered, "No, but there is wheat." Rabbi Jonathan said, "It's lentils I'm looking for." The man replied, "Would you pay such-and-such a price?" and the man quoted a price higher than the one Rabbi Jonathan's kinsman had given him. Nevertheless, Rabbi Jonathan agreed to the price. When his kinsman came back from the field, Rabbi Jonathan said to him, "Did you not tell me that lentils sold at "such-and-such a price? Your townsmen charged me a price higher than what you quoted." His kinsman asked, "You didn't mention lentils to them, did you?" Rabbi Jonathan answered, "I did." His kinsman commented, "Had you said to the men of the city, 'It's wheat I am looking for," they would have asked you, 'Would lentils do?' But since you told them, 'It's lentils I'm looking for," they asked you, 'Would you like wheat?'"

Hence it is said of such men, "They speak falsehood everyone with his neighbor; with smooth lip, and with a double heart do they speak" *[Psalm 12:3]*

Rabbi Hiyya of Sepphoris went to Sura to buy wheat. Rabbi Jonathan said to him, "When you want wheat, say, 'I am looking for barley,' and when you want barley, say, 'I am looking for wheat,' so that the price will not be increased for you." *[Midrash Tehillim 12:1; Yalkut Psalms, parag. 656)*

Notable Quotations

1. They speak falsehood everyone with his neighbor.
   With flattering lip, and with a double heart, do they speak. (12:3)

2. The words of God are pure words,
   As silver tried in a crucible on the earth, refined seven times. (12:7)

Psalm 13

Theme: This psalm is a lament of a man on the verge of death who is temporarily abandoned by God. Eventually his confidence prevails, and he promises to praise God for the deliverance from death which God he believes will ultimately grant him. Biblical commentators such as Rashi and Kimchi assert that the speaker in the psalm is none other than Israel, suffering oppression under her neighbors. The commentator Gunkel interprets the Psalm as a liturgy: verses 1-4 are uttered by the congregation; verse 5 is spoken by the priest; verses 6-8 are the response of the congregation.

Outline: 2-5 Psalmist's cry of despair
6 Revival of hope and confidence in God.

Liturgical Use: None.

Practical Use: In time of despair.

Legends: This tale is Rav Kahana's interpretation of the verse in *Psalms 13:1* "A psalm for Him who causes others to be victorious."

Rav Kahana said in the name of Rabbi Ishmael son of Rav Yose: The verse "A psalm for Him who causes others to be victorious" *[Psalm 13:1]* means: "A psalm for Him who rejoices when others are victorious over Him." Pause and consider that the behavior of the Holy Blessed One, is not like the behavior of flesh and blood. The behavior of flesh and blood: when others are victorious over him, he grieves. But when others are victorious over the Holy Blessed One, He rejoices, as is said, "Therefore God said that He would destroy them, had not Moses His chosen stood before Him in the breach" *[Psalm 106:23]. (Talmud Pesachim 119a)*

Notable Quotations

1. How long, O God, will You forget me forever?
   How long will You hide Your face from me? (13:1)

2. As for me, in Your mercy do I trust.
   My heart shall rejoice in Your salvation.
   I will sing to God,
   Because He has dealt bountifully with me. (13:6)

Psalm 14

Theme: This *Psalm*, like *Psalm 53*, is a lament. The psalmist is in profound inner distress, so weak in body as to feel near death. The commentators Rashi and Kimchi as well as several modern commentators understand this psalm as a description of the hard lot of Israel in a godless world.

Outline: 1-3 Widespread corruption
4-6 Punishment of the wicked
7 Concluding prayer

Liturgical Use: None.

Practical Use: When seeing corruption in world.

Legends: This tale, which teaches that Jacob our patriarch is the first to experience calamity, uses a verse in *Psalm 14:7* as a proof that when bounty comes to the world, Jacob is the first to feel it.

"He has burned in Jacob like a flaming fire, which then devoured round about" *[Lamentations 2:3*] Rabbi Simeon ben Lakish said: When calamity comes to the world, the first to feel it is Jacob. And the proof? "He has burned in Jacob...a fire." And when boons come to the world, the first to feel them is Jacob, as is said, "Let Jacob rejoice, let Israel be glad." *[Psalm 14:7] (Lamentations Rabbah 2:3)*

Notable Quotations

1. The fool has said in his heart: 'There is no God'.
They have dealt corruptly; they have done abominably.
There is none that does good. (14:1)

2. Oh that the salvation of Israel were come out of Zion.
When the Lord turns the captivity of His people,
Let Jacob rejoice, let Israel be glad. (14:7)

Psalm 15

Theme: Classified as a "wisdom psalm*",* *Psalm 15* is a liturgy specifying the moral qualities required for admission to the Temple. It is commonly known as 'God's Gentleman' and is descriptive of the Hebraic ideal of human character. The ancient rabbis remarked that the 613 commandments of the Torah are summarized in this psalm.

Outline: 1-5 The moral qualities of a good person.

Liturgical Use: Often used at funerals for eulogizing a good person.

Practical Use: When honoring a person of high moral capacity, *Psalm 15* would provide some outstanding quotes.

Legends: This tale of Rav Safra illustrates the verse "And speaks the truth in his heart" ***[Psalm 15:2]***

And speaks the truth in his heart" [Psalm 15:2], as for instance, Rav Safra did.

It is told of Rav Safra that he had an article to sell, and a certain man came to him while he was reciting the Shema and said, "Let me have the article for such-and-such a price." When Rav Safra did not answer, the would-be purchaser, thinking that Rav Safra was unwilling to sell for the price offered, kept increasing the amount, saying "Let me have it for more money." After Rav Safra finished the Shema, he said, "Take the article at the price you mentioned first, for I was willing to sell it to you at that price." *(Talmud Makkot 24a)*

Notable Quotations

1. He that walks uprightly and works righteousness,
And speaks the truth in his heart. (15:2)

2. That has no slander on his tongue,

Nor does evil to his fellow,
Nor takes up a reproach against his neighbor. (15:3)

3. He that does not take usurious interest,
Nor takes a bribe against the innocent,
He that does these things shall stand firm, forever. (15:5)

Psalm 16

Theme: *Psalm 16* is a hymn of utter joy and happiness through God. According to some commentators, this profession of faith was composed by a Canaanite convert to monotheism.

Outline: 1-2 Prayer and confession of faith
3-4 Psalmist's delight in the loyal and scorn of worshippers of other Gods
5-6 Psalmist's utter trust in God
7-8 Psalmist's relationship with God
9-11 Psalmist's happiness and exultant joy in God

Liturgical Use: None.

Practical Use: i. For a Jew-by-choice immediately following his or her conversion.
ii. Verse 8 "I have set the Lord always before me" is often used on the so-called *shiviti* amulet found gracing synagogue sanctuary walls.
iii. When suffering from illness. (Note: This is one of Reb Nachman of Bratslav's ten healing psalms)

Legends: This tale is about the theme of gratitude, based on the verse "My gratitude is not with you" *[Psalm 16:2]*

Rabbi Perida began his discourse with the verse "I said unto God, 'You are my God. 'My gratitude is not with you'" *[Psalm 16:2*]. The congregation of Israel said to the Holy One, "Master of the universe, show me gratitude for having made You known in the world." God replied, "My gratitude is not with you. I am grateful to none other than Abraham, Isaac and Jacob, who were first to make Me known to the world--'with the holy ones that were on the earth; they are the mighty ones in whom is all My delight'" *[Psalm 16:3] (Talmud Menachot 53a*)

Notable Quotations

1. I have said unto the Lord: 'You are my God.
   I have no good but in You. (16:2)

2. I have set the Lord always before me.
   Surely God is at my right hand, I shall not be moved. (16:8)

Psalm 17

Theme: *Psalm 17* is a prayer-lament poem in which the psalmist has been falsely accused of worshipping idols and asks for vindication.

Outline: 1-5 Plea of innocence
6-9 Psalmists prayer for protection
9-12 Portrayal of psalmist's enemies
13-14 Prayer for deliverance
15 Psalmist's sole satisfaction is God

Liturgical Use: None.

Practical Use: Anxiety from enemies

Legends: This tale is a teaching of Rabbi Dostain, who attempts to show that God's ways are different than those of man. He uses *Psalm 17:15* as his illustration.

Rabbi Dostai son of Rav Yannai preached: Pause and consider that the way of the Holy One is not like the way of flesh and blood. How does flesh and blood act? If a man brings a substantial present to the king, it may or may not be accepted. And even if it is accepted, it remains doubtful whether the man will be admitted into the king's presence. Not so with the Holy One. A man who gives but a small coin to a beggar is deemed worthy of being admitted to behold the Presence, as is written, "I shall behold Your face through charity, and when I awake, shall be satisfied with your likeness" *[Psalm 17:15]*

Rabbi Eleazar used to give a small coin to a poor man and then recite the Tefillah, because, he said, it is written, "I, through charity, shall behold Your face." *(Talmud Baba Batra 10a)*

Notable Quotations

1. Hear the right, O God, attend unto my cry.
   Give ear to my prayer from lips without deceit. (17:1)

2. Keep me as the apple of the eye,
   Hide me in the shadow of Your wings. (17:8)

3. As for me, I shall behold Your face in righteousness.
   I shall be satisfied, when I awake, with Your likeness. (17:15)

Psalm 18

Theme: *Psalm 18* is a royal psalm of thanksgiving. In the first part of the psalm, the royal poet describes his mortal peril and then depicts God's intervention. In the second half of the psalm the psalmist praises God for having trained him in war and for giving him a victory over his enemies.

Outline: 1-5 Plea of innocence
6-9 Psalmist's petition for protection
9-12 Portrayal of Psalmist's enemies
13-14 Prayer for deliverance
15 Psalmist's sole satisfaction is God

Liturgical Use: The last verse of this psalm (verse 51) "Great salvation gives God to His king, and shows mercy to His anointed, to David and his seed, for evermore is the concluding verse chosen for the Grace after the meals.

Practical Use: When feeling thankful to God.

Legends: The following legend sheds light on the verse "when you light the lamps" *[Numbers 8:2),* using by way of illustration the verse from *Psalm 18:29* "it is for you to light my lamp."

"When you light the lamps" *[Numbers 8:2*] Israel said to the Holy One: Master of the universe, are You asking us to give You light? You are the light of the world, light dwells with You, and You ask us to provide light in "front of the lampstand?" Hence, "it is for You to light my lamp" *[Psalm 18:29*]. The Holy One replied: It is not that I need your help. Still, I want you to give Me light, even as I have given you light during your wanderings.

A parable will explain God's answer. A sighted man and a blind man were walking on the way. The sighted man said to the blind man, "When we enter the house, please kindle this lamp and give me light. The blind man replied, "Out of your kindness, when I was on the road, you supported me, and until we came to the house, you accompanied me, and now you say, 'Kindle the lamp and give me light." Will you be good enough to explain why?" The sighted man answered, "The reason I asked you to give me light is to relieve you of any obligation to me for having accompanied me on the road. Hence, I said to you, 'Give me light.'" *(Numbers Rabbah 15:5)*

Notable Quotations

1. The Lord is my rock, and my fortress and my deliverer.
   My God, my rock, in Him I take refuge.
   My shield, and my horn of salvation. (18:1)

2. For You do light my lamp,
   The Lord my God does lighten my darkness. (18:29)

3. Great salvation gives God to His king.
   And he shows mercy to His anointed,
   To David and his seed, for evermore. (18:51)

Psalm 19

Theme: The witnesses to God and revelation of God in both nature and in the Law are the themes of *Psalm 19*, which falls into two distinct parts. The first seven verses are likely an adaptation to God's purposes of an ancient Canaanite hymn to the sun. Verses 8-15 constitute an instructional poem describing the excellence of the Law, often in terms which properly describe the sun.

Outline: 1-2 The language of the heavens
3-4 Celestial harmony of the spheres
5-6 Hymn to the sun
7-10 Praise and revelation of God in Torah
11-13 Psalmist's personal application of Torah to his life
14-15 Prayer for God's help.

Liturgical Use: i. Recited as part of the daily, Sabbath and festival services in the morning.
ii. The last verse of this psalm (i.e., verse 15) whose words are "Let the words of my mouth and the meditation of my heart be acceptable before You, O Lord, my Rock and my Redeemer" appears at the conclusion of the daily Amidah prayer. It is a suitable concluding prayer for the acceptance of the petitions one has just offered.

Practical Use: i. When studying the Torah.
ii. When encountering an uplifted feeling.
iii. When having doubts about one's faith.

Legends: This *midrash* is Rabbi Jacob ben Zavdi's parable about strength in which he employs an understanding of the verse "The heavens declare God's glory" *[Psalm 19:1]*.

"The heavens declare the glory of God" [*Psalm 19:1*]. Rabbi Jacob ben Zavdi told the parable of a mighty man who came to a certain city where the inhabitants did not know his strength. A knowing man said, "You can tell his strength from the size of the stone he manages to roll." Even so, we can tell the strength of the Holy Blessed One from the size of the heavens. *(Midrash Tehillim 19:6)*

Notable Quotations:

1. Day unto day utters speech,
   And night unto night reveals knowledge. (19:3)

2. The law of God is perfect, restoring the soul,
   The testimony of God is sure, making wise the simple. (19:8)

3. More (i.e., God's ordinances) to be desired are they than gold, yea, than much fine gold,
   Sweeter also than honey and the honeycomb. (19:11)

4. Let the words of my mouth and the meditation of my heart be acceptable before You,
   O Lord, my Rock and my Redeemer. (19:15)

Psalm 20

Theme: A prayer for the king before battle, this psalm is a prayer for victory and the answer to the prayer announced by a priest or prophet. The commentator Kimchi asserts that *Psalm 20* is not a Psalm by David, but rather on behalf of David, and this view is accepted by other commentators as well.

Outline: 1-5 The prayer for the king
6-8 An oracle of victory
9-10 Concluding supplication

Liturgical Use: Appears in many prayerbooks after the second rendering of *Psalm 145*, toward the conclusion of the daily morning service.

Practical Use: When petitioning God for something.

Legends: This *midrash* is in the form of a parable which illustrates the meaning of the verse "The Lord answer you in the day of trouble." *[Psalm 20:22]*

"The Lord answer you in the day of trouble" *[Psalm 20:2*] A parable of a father and son who were journeying on a road. The son, growing weary, asked his father, "Father, where is the city?" The father replied, "My son, take this as a sign: when you see a burial ground before you, then surely the city is near you." Likewise, the Holy One said to the children of Israel: When you see troubles hard by you, surely in that very hour you will be redeemed, for it is said, "The Lord will answer you in the day of trouble." *(Midrash Tehillim 20:4; Yalkut, Psalms, parag. 680.)*

Notable Quotations

1. We will shout for joy in your victory,

And in the name of our God we will set up our standards.
The Lord fulfill all your petitions. (20:6)

2. Some trust in chariots and some in horses,
But we will make mention of the name of the Lord our God. (20:8)

3. Deliver us, God.
Let the King answer us in the day that we call. (20:10)

Psalm 21

Theme: This is a psalm of thanksgiving for the royal victory prayed for in *Psalm 20*. The psalm is a two-part poem. Verses 3-8 enumerate the blessings that God has bestowed on the king. Verses 9-13 describe the battle that resulted in the victory that occasioned the writing of the psalm.

Outline: 1-7 Gratitude for God's blessings upon the King
8-13 The King addressed
14 Concluding prayer.

Liturgical Use: None

Practical Use: When wishing to offer thanksgiving because of some success.

Legends: The following is a tale which features the verse "Who is the King of Glory?"

Why did he call God "King of Glory?" Because God assigns glory to those who fear Him. The proof is that one must not ride on the horse or sit on the throne of a mortal king, yet God placed Solomon on His throne, as it says: Then Solomon sat on the throne of the Lord as king. *(I Chronicles, 29:23).* He made Elijah ride on His horse. What is the horse of God? The whirlwind and storm; as it says: The Lord, in the whirlwind and in the storm is His way, and the clouds are the dust of His feet (*Nachum 1:30,)* and it is written: And Elijah went up by a whirlwind into heaven *(II Kings 2:11).* One must not make use of the scepter of a mortal king, but God handed His scepter to Moses, as it says: And Moses took the rod of God in his hand. *(Exodus 4:20).* One must not wear the crown of a mortal king, but God will one day place His crown on the Messiah, the King. Of what is the crown of God? Of very fine gold, as it says: His head is as the finest gold, his locks are curled, and black as a raven. *(Song of*

Songs 5:11), and it is written: You set a crown of fine gold on his head. *(Psalm 21:4) (Exodus Rabbah, Va'era, 8:1)*

Notable Quotations:

1. For You meet him with choice blessings.
   You set a crown of fine gold on his head. (21:4)

2. Your hand shall be equal to all your enemies.
   Your right hand shall overtake those that hate you. (21:9)

3. Be exalted O God, in Your strength.
   So we will sing and praise Your power. (21:14)

Psalm 22

Theme: A poem of lament in which the psalmist complains of his sufferings and tries to move God to help him. The psalmist makes a vow to praise God in the great assembly.

Outline: 1-2 Psalmist feels forsaken by God
3-5 Psalmist's appeal to history
6-11 Contrast of Psalmist's shame with the deliverance of his fathers
12-18 Plea to God
23-32 Gratitude and praise

Liturgical Use: None

Practical Use: i. Anxiety from enemies
ii. When needing to increase one's trust in God.
iii. When feeling threatened, anxious or afraid
iv. Feeling humiliated by people.

Legends: This is a tale about Esther and Mordecai, promulgated by the verse in *Psalm 22:* 1 "For the Leader, upon the hind of the dawn."

In the verse "For the Leader, upon the hind of the dawn" (*Psalm 22:1*), Scripture speaks of the generation of Mordecai and Esther, [a time that was darker than the night.] For though it is night, one has the light of the moon, the stars, and the planets. Then when is it really dark? Just before dawn. After the moon sets and the stars set and the planets vanish, there is no darkness deeper than the hour before dawn, and in that hour the Holy One answers the world and all that is in it: out of the darkness, He brings forth the dawn and gives light to the world.

Then, too, why is Esther compared to the hind of the dawn? What is true of the light of dawn? Its light rays out as it rises. At the beginning, light comes little by little. Then it spreads wider and wider, grows and increases; and at last, it bursts into shining glory. So too, Israel's redemption through Esther came about little by little. At the beginning "Mordecai sat in the king's gate" *[Esther 2:21*]; then "the king saw Esther the queen" *[Esther 5:2];* then "on that night the king could not sleep" *[Esther 6:1];* then "Haman took the apparel and the horse" *[Esther 6:11*]; then "they hanged Haman" *[Esther 7:10];* then Ahasuerus said to Esther and Mordecai, "Write concerning the Jews as you see fit" *[Esther 8:80*]; then "Mordecai went forth from the presence of the king in royal apparel" *[Esther 8:15*]; and at last "the Jews had light and gladness" *[Esther 8:16)*

The sages said: When a hind is thirsty, she digs a hole, fixes her horns in it, and in her distress cries softly to the Holy One. The Holy One causes the deep to come up, and the deep causes water to spring up for her. So, too, Esther: when wicked Haman decreed cruel decrees against Israel, she, in her distress, began to softly cry in prayer to the Holy One, and the Holy One answered her.

Rav Assi said: As the dawn ends the night, so all miracles recorded in the Bible ended with Esther. *(Midrash Tehillim 22:13; Talmud Yoma, 29a)*

Notable Quotations

1. My God, my God, why have Your forsaken me,
   And are far from my help at the words of my cry? (22:2)

2. I will declare Your name to my brethren.
   Amid the congregation will I praise You. (22:23)

3. Let the humble eat and be satisfied.
   Let them praise God that seeks after Him.
   May your heart be quickened forever. (22:27)

Psalm 23

Theme: One of the most famous of all the Book of Psalms, *Psalm 23* is a psalm of trust and confidence. God is the psalmist's shepherd and will guide him through all his trials of this life to the eternal bliss of the world to come.

Outline: 1-3 God as Shepherd Provider
4-6 God as Shepherd Provider and Host

Liturgical Use: Appears in numerous prayerbooks in the Yizkor Memorial Prayer service, recited on behalf of deceased loved ones on the holy days of Yom Kippur, Shemini Atzeret, Passover and Shavuot. Also often recited at funerals or burial services, since it is a poem of comfort.

Practical Use: i. Anxiety concern about livelihood
ii. When in need to increase one's trust in God.
iii. When feeling threatened, anxious, or afraid.

Legends: This legend is in answer to Rabbi Isaac's question concerning to whom the verse "Yea, though I walk through the valley of the shadow of death...." refers.

Rabbi Isaac said: To whom does the verse "Yea, though I walk through the valley of the shadow of death, I will fear no evil, for You are with me" *[Psalm 23:4*] refer? To him who sleeps in the shadow of a single date palm or in a shadow produced by the moon.

Four kinds of shade are haunted by demons: the shade of a single date palm, the shade of a kinnara, the shade of a caper, and the shade of thorny bushes whose fronds are made edible. Some say, also the shade of a ship, and the shade of a willow. This is the general rule: Whatever has many branches, its shade is dangerous; and whatever has hard thorns, its shade is dangerous. The exception is the thorny bush whose fronds are made edible; its shade is not dangerous, even though its thorns are hard, for Shida (female demon) said to her son, "Stay away from the thorny bush whose fronds are made edible, because that is the one that killed your father."

In a place of capers, there are spirits. In a place of thorny bushes with edible fronds, there are demons. On rooftops, there are fiery bolt demons. What are the practical consequences? In the writing of an amulet, it is important to know the identity of the agent who caused the injury.

A thorny bush with edible fronds near a town is haunted by no fewer than sixty demons. What is the practical consequence? In the writing of an amulet, it is necessary to know the number of demons who caused the injury.

When the prefect of a certain city went and stood by a thorny bush with edible fronds near the city, he was set upon by sixty demons, and his life was in danger. So, he went to a certain sage who did not know that it was a thorny bush with edible fronds haunted by sixty demons, and so he wrote a one-demon amulet for it. Then he heard the demons dancing in the tree and singing, "Though this sage's head scarf is like a sage's, we have examined him and find that he does not know how to make the blessing before putting on such a scarf." Then another sage came who knew that the cause was the thorny bush with edible fronds that is haunted by sixty demons, and he wrote a sixty-demon amulet for the prefect's injury. Then he heard the demons say, "Clear your vessels away from here." *(Talmud Pesachim 11a-b)*

Notable Quotations

A Psalm of David,
The Lord is my shepherd, I shall not want.
He causes me to lie down in green pastures,
And leads me beside the still waters.
He restores my soul.
He guides me in straight paths for His name's sake.

Yea, though I walk through the valley of the shadow of death,
I will fear no evil,
For You are with me.
Your rod and Your staff, they comfort me.
You prepare a table before me in the presence of my enemies,
You have anointed my head with oil, my cup overflows.
Surely goodness and mercy shall follow me all the days of my life,
And I will dwell in the house of the Lord forever. (23: 1-6)

Psalm 24

Theme: This is a psalm used on connection with a procession of the ark. When King David defeated the Jebusites, he brought the ark of the covenant to Jerusalem. This psalm was likely composed for the joyous occasion. According to tradition, *Psalm 24* was regularly recited in the Temple on the first day of the week. Today, it appears in every prayerbook as the Psalm for Sunday.

Outline: 1-2 Poem celebrating God the Creator
3-6 Liturgy of entrance for worshippers
7-10 Entrance of the ark into the Temple

Liturgical Use: Recited each week on Sunday, *Psalm 24* is the Psalm for Sunday. In addition, *Psalm 24* is also recited when the Torah scroll is returned to the ark on a festival which occurs during the week.

Practical Use: When sensing an uplifted feeling.

Legends: This legend attempts to identify the names of the seas on the verse in *Psalm 24:2* "He has founded it upon the seas and established it upon the floods.'

When Rav Dimi came to the Land, Rabbi Yochanan said: The verse "He has founded it upon the seas and established it upon the floods" *[Psalm 24:2]* refers to the seven seas and four rivers that surround the Land of Israel. The seven seas: Sea of Tiberias, Sea of Sodom, Sea of Elat, Sea of Shalit, Sea of Samachonitis, Sea of Apamea, and the Great Mediterranean Sea. The four rivers: the Jordan, the Yarmuk, the Keramiyon and the Pisgah.

But is there not also the Sea of Emessa? No, because Diocletian brought the waters of several rivers together to form that sea. (*Talmud Baba Batra 74b; Jerusalem Talmud Kilayim 9:4; Jerusalem Talmud Ketubot 12:3; Midrash Tehillim 24:6)*

Notable Quotations

1. The earth is the Lords, and the fullness thereof,
The world, and they that dwell therein. (24:1)

2. Who shall ascend the mountain of God,
Who shall stand in his holy place? (24:3)

3. Lift up your heads, O you gates,
And be you lifted up, you everlasting doors,
That the King of Glory may enter. (24:7)

Psalm 25

Theme: This poem is an individual lament in acrostic form, each successive verse beginning with another letter of the Hebrew alphabet. It is an appeal on the part of the psalmist for protection and guidance.

Outline: 1-7 Utterance of trust and petition
8-14 Praise of God
16-21 Psalmist's petitions
22 Concluding petition about redemption

Liturgical Use: None

Practical Use: i. After committing a sin
ii. Anxiety from enemies
iii. Feeling religiously confused.

Legends: This is a tale which deals with the tortures of Hadrian's generation, of which David makes a comment in the opening verse of *Psalm 25.*

Rabbi Hiyya bar Abba said: If someone told me, "Give up our life for the hallowing of the Name of the Holy One," I would give it up, provided I were put to death at once. But I could not endure the tortures of the generation of Hadrian's persecution.

What was done to people during that generation? Iron balls would be brought, heated white in fire, then wedged into their armpits until they gave up their souls. Or sharpened reeds were brought and driven in under their fingernails until they gave up their souls. Of such torture, David said, "Unto You, O God, do I lift up my soul" *[Psalm 25:1*]. It is written *assi*, ("I give up"), indicating that they gave up their souls for the hallowing of the Holy One's Name. *(Song of Songs Rabbah 2:7, parag. 1)*

Notable Quotations

1. Show me Your ways, O God,
   Teach me Your paths. (25:4)

2. God guides those who are humble in justice,
   And God teaches the humble His way. (25:9)

3. Turn to me and be gracious
   For I am alone and afflicted. (25:16)

Psalm 26

Theme: This is a psalm of innocence and plea of the upright. Accused of idol worship, the psalmist responds with a plea for judgment, a protestation of innocence, a prayer to God and a reaffirmation of his innocence.

Outline: 1-3 Psalmist opens his integrity to God's scrutiny
4-8 Psalmist's self-vindication
9-12 Psalmist's prayer is renewed

Liturgical Use: Verse 26:8 "Lord, I love the habitation of Your house, and the place where Your glory dwells" appears as one of the verses in the *Ma Tovu* opening prayer, which sets the psychological mood for the worshippers.

Practical Use: Upon entering the synagogue sanctuary.

Legends: This short tale concerns the importance and greatness of peace, using a verse in *Psalm 26* as its illustration.

"And the Land shall yield her produce" *[Leviticus 26:4].* You might say, "Well, we've got food, we've got drink." Still, if there is no peace, there is nothing at all, for the Bible goes on to say, "And I will give peace in the Land" *[Psalm 26:6],* which indicates that peace equals all else. Indeed, we say in the morning Tefillah, "When God made peace, God made everything." *(Sifre Leviticus, ed. Weiss, p. 111a)*

Notable Quotations

1. Examine me, O God, and try me.
   Test my reigns and my heart. (26:2)

2. I hate the gathering of evil doers,

And will not sit with the wicked. (26:5)

3. Lord, I love the habitation of Your house,
   And the place where Your glory dwells. (26:8)

Psalm 27

Theme: This hymn of confidence demonstrates the Psalmist's fearless trust in God, who is confident of God's protection in this life and is also convinced that he will gaze upon the loveliness of God in the world to come.

Outline: 1-3 Psalmists unconditional confidence in God
4-6 God is the Psalmist's protector
7-14 Call for help

Liturgical Use: The Code of Jewish Law requires this psalm to be recited each morning and evening beginning with the month of Elul (prior to the Jewish New Year of *Rosh Hashanah*) and lasting until *Hoshanna Rabbah*. The enemies in verse 12 of this psalm are metaphorically interpreted as the promptings to sin from which deliverance is sought.

Practical Use: i. In the synagogue
ii. When feeling abandoned.

Legends: This very short tale, using a verse in *Psalm 27* as an illustration, explains the importance of continual prayer.

Rav Hama bar Hanina said: If a man sees that he prays and is not answered, he should pray again, for Scripture says, "Wait for the Lord, be strong and let your heart take courage, yea, wait for the Lord" *[Psalm 27:14) (Talmud Berachot 32b)*

Notable Quotations

1. The Lord is my light and salvation, whom shall I fear,
The Lord is the stronghold of my life, of whom shall I be afraid.
(27:1)

2. One thing have I asked of God, that will I seek after,
That I may dwell in the house of God all the days of my life. (27:4)

3. Hear O God, when I call with my voice,
Be gracious to me, and answer. (27:7)

4. Deliver me not over to the will of my adversaries.
For false witnesses are risen against me, and such as breathe out violence. (27:12)

5. Wait for God,
Be strong, and let your heart take courage,
Yea, wait for God. (27:14)

Psalm 28

Theme: This psalm consists of two distinct but related parts. Verses 1-5 give expression to a personal lament for deliverance from imminent death, while verses 6-9 are a hymn of thanksgiving for the recovery from a serious illness.

Outline: 1-2 Introductory appeal
3-5 Psalmist's petition that his fate may not be that of the wicked
6-7 Psalmist's prayer heard
8-9 Prayer for the people

Liturgical Use: Verse 28 "Save Your people, and bless Your inheritance, and tend them and carry them forever" appears several times in the prayerbook. Most notably it appears at the end of the Hoshannot verses to God. On Hoshanna Rabbah, the custom is to beat the willow twigs against the floor, causing leaves to fall, symbolizing that we can separate sin from our lives. This procedure is followed by the singing of verse 28: "Save Your people..."

Practical Use: After recovering from an illness

Legends: This one-line statement attempts to explain the verse in *Psalms 28:5* "Because they do not regard the works of the Lord, nor the operation of His hands."

"Because they regard not the works of the Lord, nor the operation of His hands" *[Psalm* 28:5]. This applies, according to Rabbi Joshua ben Levi, to men who have no regard for *Aggadot. (Midrash Tehillim 28:5)*

Notable Quotations

1. Hear the voice of my supplications, when I cry to You,
   When I lift up my hands toward Your holy sanctuary. (28:2)

2. Blessed be God,
   Because He has heard the voice of my supplications. (28:6)

3. Save your people and bless Your inheritance.
   And tend them and carry them forever. (28:9)

Psalm 29

Theme: God's manifestation in nature and His majesty in the storm is the theme of *Psalm 29.* According to the Talmud *(Berachot 29a*), the seven Sabbath blessings correspond to the "seven voices of God" mentioned in this Psalm.

Outline: 1-2 Prelude
3-9 Seven voices of God
10-11 God is Ruler and King over Israel

Liturgical Use: The Psalm is included in the Sabbath liturgy as part of the *Kabbalat Shabbat* service on Friday evening. It is also recited on Sabbath mornings during the service for returning the Torah scroll to the holy ark.

Practical Use: Recite during a thunderstorm

Legends: This tale attempts to prove the point that a worshipper ought not to recite the *Tefillah* except in a reverent frame of mind. It uses verse 2 in *Psalm 29* as the proof text.

One should not stand up to say the Tefillah except in a reverent frame of mind. The pious men of yore used to spend an hour in meditation and pray only after that, to make sure that their hearts would be directed to their Father in heaven.

And the proof from Scripture? From the verse "Worship the Lord in the beauty (*hadrat)* of holiness" *[Psalm 29:2],* concerning which Rabbi Joshua ben Levi said, Read not *hadra*t but *herda*t [awe]. But Rabbi Nachman bar Isaac said, From another verse: "Serve the Lord with fear and rejoice with trembling" *[Psalm 2:11],* which according to Rav means: Where there is rejoicing, there is also to be trembling. *(Talmud Berachot 30b)*

Notable Quotations

1. The voice of God is upon the water.
   The God of glory thunders,
   Even the Lord upon many waters. (29:3)

2. The voice of the Lord makes the hinds to calve,
   And strips the forests bare.
   And in His temple all say: 'Glory.' (29:9)

3. Adonai will give strength to His people,
   Adonai will bless God's people with peace. (29:11)

Psalm 30

Theme: A psalm of thanksgiving for recovery from an illness that brought the psalmist to death's door. Because of the superscription of the Psalm (i.e., A Song at the Dedication of the House of David), it has been conjectured that the psalm was used for the dedication of David's palace. *(II Samuel 5:11)*

Outline: 2-6 Gratitude for recovery
7-11 Psalmist relates his experience
12-13 Psalmist's prayer is answered.

Liturgical Use: Used daily in the preliminary service before the prayer "Baruch She'amar."

Practical Use: i. When feeling sad or depressed
ii. After recovering from an illness

Legends: Following is a legend related to first fruits in which the Levites are said to sing the second verse of *Psalm 30* as part of the pageantry.

How are the first fruits taken to Jerusalem? All the inhabitants of the towns that make up a lay post assemble in the city of the head of that post but spend the night in its open place without entering any of the houses. Early in the morning, the head of the post says, "Let us arise and go up to Zion, unto the house of the Lord our God" *[Jeremiah 31:6]*.

Those who live near Jerusalem bring fresh figs and grapes, but those from a distance bring dried figs and raisins. Before them walks an ox, its horn overlaid with gold, a crown of olive leaves on its head. A flute strikes the tempo for their procession until they approach Jerusalem. When they arrive close to Jerusalem, they send messengers to announce their coming. Meanwhile, they arrange their first fruits in an ornamental display. Governors of priests, chiefs of the Levites, and treasures of the Temple go out to meet them. The number of those going out varies in keeping with the number of the entrants. All the skilled artisans of Jerusalem are required to rise before them and greet them: "Brethren, men of such-and-such a place, peace be upon you in your coming."

The flute continues to strike the tempo before them until they reach the Temple Mount. When they reach the Temple Mount, even King Agrippa places a basket on his shoulder and walks as far as the Temple Court. As they approach the Temple Court, the Levites sing, "I will extol You, O God, for You have raised me up, and have not suffered my enemies to rejoice over me." *[Psalm 30:2] (Talmud Bikkurim 3)*

Notable Quotations

1. I will extol you O God, for You have raised me up,
   And have not suffered my enemies to rejoice over me. (30:2)

2. For His anger is but for a moment,
   His favor is for a lifetime
   Weeping may tarry at night,
   But joy always come with the dawn. (30:6)

3. You did turn for me my mourning into dancing.
   You did loose my sackcloth and gird me with gladness. (30:12)

Psalm 31

Theme: A personal lament, in which the psalmist cries for help. After describing the mental anguish of the psalmist, the psalm concludes with a hymn of thanksgiving for rescue from both death and slander.

Outline: 2-9 Prayer of faith
10-19 Distress of the Psalmist
20-22 Psalmist's confession of confidence
23-25 Praise for deliverance

Liturgical Use: Verse 6 "Into Your hand do I commit my spirit" is the theme of the concluding lines of the synagogue hymn Adon Olam.

Practical Use: i. Anxieties from enemies
ii. Great troubles and distress

Legends: **Following *is a midrash* about God's work and God's rest at the time of creation. Verse 20 of *Psalm 31* is used as one of the scriptural references.**

Rabbi Pinchas said in the name of Rav Hoshaia: Although you read, "Because on it He rested from all His work" *[Genesis 2:3],* He rested, to be sure, from the work of creating His world. But not from the work of the wicked and the work of the righteous, for He works with the former and with the latter. He shows the ones the consequences of their essential character and the others the consequences of their essential character. How do we know that the punishment of the wicked is called work? Because it is said, "The Lord has opened His armory, and has brought forth the weapons of His indignation, for it is a work that the Lord God has to do" *[Jeremiah 50:25].* And how do we know that the bestowing of reward upon the righteous is called work? Because it is said, "Oh, how abundant is Your goodness, which You have laid up for them that fear You, which You have worked for them that take refuge in You" *[Psalm 31:20] (Genesis Rabbah 11:10; Yalkut, Jeremiah, parag. 35)*

Notable Quotations

1. You are my rock and my fortress.
   Therefore, for Your name's sake lead me and guide me. (31:4)

2. Into your hand I commit my spirit.
   You have redeemed me, O God, You God of truth. (31:6)

3. Be strong and let your heart take courage,
   All you that wait for God. (31:25)

Psalm 32

Theme: A psalm of thanksgiving for recovery from illness. Since disease was believed to have been the result of transgression, healing is proof that transgression is forgiven. *Psalm 32* is one of the ten healing psalms of Rabbi Nachman of Bratzlav.

Outline: 2 Happy is the pardoned sinner
3-4 Psalmist's distress before confession
5 Way to health and peace
6 Practical lesson of Psalmist's experience
8-9 The Psalmist turns sage
10-11 The lot of the godless and the loyal

Liturgical Use: Appears in many High Holy Day prayerbooks as a *Psalm of Atonement* in the preliminary service for *Yom Kippur*, the Day of Atonement.

Practical Use: After committing a sin.

Legends: This tale defines "hard times" in verse 6 of *Psalm 32*: "Let every pious man pray unto You when hard times fall."

"Therefore, let every pious man pray to You when hard times fall" *[Psalm 32:6]*. "Hard times" means old age according to Rabbi Abba. Concerning his old age, a man should pray that his eyes continue to see, his mouth to eat, and his feet to walk. For when a man grows old, all his functions desert him. (*Tanchuma Miketz, parag. 10)*

Notable Quotations

1. Happy is the person unto whom God counts not iniquity,
And in whose spirit there is no guile. (32:2)

2. Many are the sorrows of the wicked,
   But he that trusts in God, mercy compasses him about. (32:10)

3. Be glad in God, and rejoice you righteous,
   And shout for joy, all you that are upright in heart. (32:11)

Psalm 33

Theme: A hymn of triumph and a song of national deliverance.

Outline: 1-3 Introductory invocation
4-11 Reasons for why praise is due
12-19 God's chosen people
20-22 The people's response

Liturgical Use: Is recited during weekday preliminary service.

Practical Use: When feeling thankful.

Legends: Rabbi Eleazar's comments on charity and justice are theme of this *midrash,* which uses several illustrative verses from the Book of Psalms.

Rabbi Eleazar said further: He who executes charity and justice is as though he had filled the entire world, all of it, with lovingkindness, as is said, "When one loves charity and justice, the earth is full of the loving-kindness of God" *[Psalm 33:5].* Should you suppose that one may achieve this easily, Scripture says, "How rare is Your loving-kindness, O God" *[Psalm 36:].* Should you suppose that difficulty in executing charity and justice is also true of one who fears Heaven, Scripture says, "But the lovingkindness of God is from everlasting to everlasting with those who fear God" *[Psalm 103:17]. (Talmud Sukkah 49b)*

Notable Quotations

1. Give thanks to God with harp,
   Sing praises to God with the psaltery of ten strings. (33:2)

2. For God spoke and it was.
   God commanded and it stood. (33:9)

3. Our soul has waited for God.
   God is our help and our shield. (33:20)

Psalm 34

Theme: An alphabetical acrostic, *Psalm 34* is a psalm of thanksgiving. The grateful psalmist invites others who are afflicted to join him in this hymn of praise to God.

Outline: 1-3 An invitation to praise
4-7 Psalmist's experience with God
8-10 The Psalmist turns evangelist
11-22 Psalmist turns sage

Liturgical Use: Is recited daily, appearing in the daily morning preliminary service.

Practical Use: When experiencing great troubles and distress.

Legends: This peddler's tale employs the verse in *Psalm 34:13* in trying to determine the elixir of life.

The story of a peddler who went around the villages of Sepphoris, hawking his wares, crying, "Who'd like the elixir of life?" Everybody gathered around and implored him, "Give us the elixir of life." While seated in his reception chamber, busily explaining the literal meaning of Scripture, Rav Yannai heard the peddler crying, "Who'd like the elixir of life?" He called out, "Come up here and sell it to me." The peddler answered: "Not to you or to the likes of you." But Yannai insisted, so the peddler came up to him, took out a book of Psalms, and showed him the verse "Who is the man that desires life?" *[Psalm 34:13*] and what is written after it: "Keep your tongue from evil." As he read these words, Rav Yannai remarked, "Solomon also proclaimed the same when he said, "Whoso keeps his mouth and his tongue keeps his soul from troubles,"". [*Proverbs 21:23*]

Then Rabbi Yannai added, "All my days I have been reading this verse, but I did not realize its plain meaning until this peddler came by and made me aware of it." *(Leviticus Rabbah 16:2; Talmud*

Avodah Zarah 19b)

Notable Quotations

1. I will bless God at all times.
   His praise shall continually be in my mouth. (34:1)

2. Come you children, and listen to me,
   I will teach you the fear of God. (34:12)

3. Who is the person that desires life,
   And loves days that he may see good therein?
   Keep your tongue from evil,
   And your lips from speaking guile. (34: 13-14)

4. God is near to them that are of a broken heart,
   And saves such as are of a contrite spirit. (34:19)

Psalm 35

Theme: A cry of distress from David when he was being hunted down by King Saul.

Outline: 1-10 Appeal for help
11-18 Wickedness of the enemy
19-28 Psalmist's final plea

Liturgical Use: None

Practical Use: i. Anxiety from enemies.
ii. When betrayed or hurt by others.

Legends: This tale about hostility employs the verse in *Psalm 35:10* "Who is like unto You, who delivers the wretched..."

"When a man's ways please God, He makes even those hostile to him be at peace with him" *[Proverbs 16:7*]. Rabbi Joshua ben Levi said: The words "those hostile to him" refer to the impulse to evil. In the way of the world, when a man grows up in a city with another for two or three years, he is bound to the other in affection. But this one, though it grows up with a man from youth to old age, its hostile nature is such that if it is with him for even seventy years, it will bring him down. And even if it is with him for eighty years, it will still bring him down. In David's question "Who is like unto You, who delivers the wretched...and the needy from his despoiler*?" [Psalm 35:10],* Rav Acha identified "his despoiler" by asking, "Is there a despoiler greater than the impulse to evil?" (*Genesis Rabbah 54:1)*

Notable Quotations

1. My soul shall be joyful in God,
   It shall rejoice in God's salvation. (35:9)

2. God, how long will You look on?
Rescue my soul from their destructions,
My only one from the lions. (35:17)

3. My tongue shall speak of Your righteousness,
And of Your praise all day. (35:28)

Psalm 36

Theme: The main theme of this psalm is the attributes of God, in particular God's love for His creatures. God's glory is made more prominent in comparison to the sinfulness of the wicked.

Outline: 2-5 Portrait of the godless
6-10 Attributes of God.
11-13 Concluding prayer

Liturgical Use: None

Practical Use: Use when frustrated at wickedness of people.

Legends: This tale utilizes the verse in *Psalm 36:7* "They who practice Your righteousness are like the mighty mountains" to describe how the righteous bear fruit while the wicked yield none.

"They who practice Your righteousness are like the mighty mountains" *[Psalm 36:7]* As the mountains are sown and yield fruit, so the deeds of the righteous yield fruit which benefits them and others. By what parable may the matter be illustrated? By that of a golden ball whose clapper is a pearl. "They upon whom Your judgments are imposed are like the greet deep"--these are the wicked. As the deep cannot be sown to yield fruit, so the deeds of the wicked cannot yield fruit, for if they yielded fruit, they would destroy the world. (*Tanchuma Emor, parag. 5)*

Notable Quotations

1. Your lovingkindness, O God, is in the heavens,
   Your faithfulness reaches unto the skies. (36:6)

2. For with You is the fountain of life.

In Your light do we see light. (36:10)

Psalm 37

Theme: This poem, written as an acrostic, is one of the so-called wisdom psalms. It is concerned with thoughts concerning the seeming triumph of evil. We learn that in His own time, God punishes the wicked and rewards the righteous. This psalm attempts to counsel and encourage all of those depressed with the apparent success of not-so-good people.

Outline: 1-11 Admonitions for periods of stress and strain
12-20 Destiny of the sinful
21-31 God's considerate care of the faithful
32-40 Observance of the retributive principle.

Liturgical Use: Verse 25 "I have been young, and now am old, yet I have not seen the righteous forsaken, nor his seed begging bread" appears and is recited at the conclusion of the *Birkat Hamazon*, the Blessing after the Meal. It is most often recited at meals on the Sabbath and Festivals.

Practical Use: When confused by the success of the wicked and envious of the rich.

Legends: This is a psalm about a person that contends with the wicked people in the world. It uses *Proverbs 28:4* "Contend not with evildoers..." as one of its scriptural proof texts.

Rabbi Dostai son of Rabbi Mattan said: It is permitted to contend with the wicked in the world, as is said, "They that forsake the Torah praise the wicked; but such as keep the Torah contend with them" *[Proverbs 28:4*]. Should someone whisper to you, "Contend not with evildoers, neither be envious of them that work unrighteousness" [*Psalm 37:1],* say to him, "One who is afraid of the secular authorities speaks in such a way. As for the verse in the psalm, it is to be read, 'Strive not with evildoers" by trying to be like evildoers, and 'neither be envious of them that work unrighteousness' by trying to be like those who work unrighteousness."

But Rabbi Isaac said: If you see a wicked man upon whom the hour smiles, do not contend with him. *(Talmud Berachot 7b)*

Notable Quotations

1. Commit your way unto God.
   Trust in God and God will bring it to pass. (37:5)

2. Better is a little that the righteous have
   Than the abundance of many wicked. (37:16)

3. I have been young, and now am old.
   Yet I have not seen the righteous forsaken,
   Nor his seed begging bread. (37:25)

4. Mark the man of integrity and behold the upright.
   For there is a future for the person of peace. (37:37)

Psalm 38

Theme: In this individual lament, (written with an alphabetical structure of 22 verses) the psalmist is gravely ill. The common belief that illness was a punishment for one's transgressions provided an excellent opportunity to the foes of the psalmist, who were eager to slander him.

Outline: 2-9 Suffering of psalmist
1-15 Suffering intensified by friends and enemies
16-23 Psalmist's plea to God

Liturgical Use: None

Practical Use: Anxiety from one's enemies.

Legends: This tale is a commentary on the verse in *The Book of Genesis* "The word of God came to Abram in a vision."

Prophecy is expressed by ten designations: prophecy, vision, preaching, speech, saying, command, burden, parable, metaphor and enigma. Which is the severest form? Rabbi Leazar said: Vision, as it says, "A grievous vision is declared to me. [*Isaiah 21:2*]. Rabbi Yochanan said: Speech (*dibbur*), as it says, "the man, the lord of the land, spoke (*dibber*) roughly with us. *[Genesis 42:30*] The Rabbis said: Burden, as it says, "As a heavy burden." (*Psalm 38:5*). Great then was the power of Abraham that Divine converse was held with him in vision and speech. *(Genesis Rabbah, Lech Lecha, 44:6)*

Notable Quotations

1. Your arrows are gone deep into me,
And Your hand is come down upon me. (38:3)

2. For in You, O God, do I hope.

For You will answer, O Lord my God. (38:16)

3. Forsake me not, O God.
   O my God, be not far from me. (38:22)

Psalm 39

Theme: A lament in which the psalmist prays for healing from a serious illness. The psalmist asks for deliverance from his affliction.

Outline: 1-3 The Psalmist keeping himself in control
4-6 The Psalmist's melancholy resignation
7-12 Psalmist's prayer for relief
13-14 Final Plea

Liturgical Use: None

Practical Use: After having been slandered, abused verbally or a victim of wrongdoing.

Legends: This tale is an incident in the life of Mar Ukba, who sends a question to Rabbi Eleazar regarding his enemies.

After becoming exilarch, Mar Ukba sent a query to Rabbi Eleazar: "Certain men are against me, but I am able to get them into trouble with the government. Shall I do so?" Rabbi Eleazar scribbled his answer on the same paper: "I said, 'I will take heed to my ways, that I sin not with my tongue; I will keep a curb upon my mouth, while the wicked is before me' *[Psalm 39:2*], meaning, ever though the wicked is before me, I will still keep a curb on my mouth." Mar Ukba sent another message to Rabbi Eleazar: "They are troubling me very much, and I no longer can put up with them." Eleazar replied, "'Resign yourself to God, and wait patiently (*hit'hole*l] for him' [*Psalm 37:7].* That is to say, he added, "Wait for God, and He will utterly prostrate them [*halalim*] before you. Pay them no need, go to the house of study morning and evening, and they, by their own doing, will soon come to an end." Rabbi Eleazar had hardly written these words when Geniva (i.e., one of Mar Ukba's chief opponents) was placed in chains for execution. *(Talmud Gittin 7a)*

Notable Quotations

1. Lord, make me to know my end,
And the measure of my days, what it is.
Let me know how short-lived I am. (39:5)

2. And now, God, what do I wait for?
My hope, it is in You. (39:8)

3. Hear my prayer, O God, and give ear to my cry.
Keep not silence at my tears.
For I am a stranger with You,
A sojourner, as all my ancestors were. (39:13)

Psalm 40

Theme: A composite psalm of two parts, verses 2-11 are a hymn of thanksgiving for healing from a severe illness, while verses 12-17 (almost identical with *Psalm 70),* are a lament and petition for aid in present danger.

Outline: 2-4 Psalmist's trust in God rewarded
5-6 Happiness of those who trust
7-9 How gratitude is best displayed
10-12 Public testimony to God's righteousness
13-18 Plea for help.

Liturgical Use: None

Practical Use: Desirous to repent.

Legends: This tale attempts to answer the question regarding how many scrolls make up what is the sacred Torah scroll.

Rabbi Yochanan said in the name of Rabbi Banaah: The Torah was given in separate scrolls, for David declared, "Then I said, who am alluded to in a scroll in the book of Torah, am come" [*Psalm 40:8]*. But Rabbi Simeon ben Lakish said: The Torah was given as one sealed book, for it is said, "When Moses had finished writing the words of this Torah in a book, to the very end, Moses commanded the Levites, 'Take this book of Torah'" *[Deuteronomy 31;26*] *(Talmud Gittin 60a)*

Notable Quotations

1. I waited patiently for God.
   And He inclined unto me and heard my cry. (40:2)

2. Happy is the person that has made God his trust,

And has not turned unto the arrogant, nor unto such as fall away treacherously. (40:5)

3. Be pleased, O God, to deliver me.
   O God, make haste to help me. (40:14)

Psalm 41

Theme: A sufferer's prayer, this psalm is a prayer for healing from sickness which closes with a prayer for eternal life with God. Psalm 41 is one of the so-called ten healing Psalms of Rabbi Nachman of Bratzlav.

Outline: 2-4 Blessedness of the benevolent
5-10 Malice of Psalmist's enemies
11-12 Psalmist's prayer has been heard
14 Closing doxology to end Book I of the Book of Psalms

Liturgical Use: None

Practical Use: i. When betrayed, hurt by others or someone close
ii. When in need of healing

Legends: This tale is a commentary on the verse in Psalms "Happy is he that considers the poor" ***[Psalm 41:2]***

Happy is he that considers the poor" *[Psalm 41:2*]: Consider carefully how to benefit him. When Rabbi Jonah saw a man of good family who had lost his money and was ashamed to accept charity, he would go and say to him, "I have heard that an inheritance has come your way in a city across the sea. So here is an article of some value. Sell it and use the proceeds. When you are more affluent, you will repay me." As soon as the man took it, Rabbi Jonah would say, "It's yours as a gift." (*Leviticus Rabbah 34:1; Jerusalem Talmud Peah 8:8, 21b)*

Notable Quotations

1. Happy is the one who considers the poor,
The Lord will deliver him in the day of evil. (41:2)

2. The Lord support him on the bed of illness.
   May You turn all his lying down in his sickness. (41:4)

3. Blessed be the Lord, the God of Israel,
   From everlasting to everlasting, Amen and Amen. (41:14)

Psalm 42

Theme: The psalmist finds himself in a state of extreme desolation because God has withdrawn His spiritual favors. *Psalm 42* is the psalmist's lament.

Outline: 2-3 Psalmists yearning for communion with God
4-6 Distressed by past memories
7-8 Plight of the Psalmist
9-12 Joyful memories contrasted with the painful present

Liturgical Use: Appears in several prayerbooks as a psalm for a house of mourning.

Practical Use: When sad or depressed.

Legends: This tale concerns a Resh Lakish statement which asserts that when a man occupies himself with Torah at night, God will extend to him a thread of grace during the day.

Resh Lakish said: When a man occupies himself with Torah in the night, the Holy One extends to him a thread of grace during the day, as is said, "By day the Lord will command His lovingkindness and in the night His song shall be with me" *[Psalm 42:9]*. Why will "the Lord command His loving-kindness by day?" Because "God's song is with me in the night." *(Talmud Avodah Zarah 3b)*

Notable Quotations

1. My soul thirsts for God, for the living God,
   When shall I come and appear before God? (42:3)

2. Why are you cast down, O my soul,

And why do you moan within me?
Hope in God, for I shall yet praise Him
For the salvation of His countenance. (42:6)

3. By day God will command His lovingkindness,
And in the night God's song shall be with me,
Even a prayer unto the God of my life. (42:9)

Psalm 43

Theme: A prayer of exile, a supplement to psalm 42.

Outline: 1-2 Plea for vindication
3-4 Prayer for returning home.
5 Closing refrain

Liturgical Use: None.

Practical Use: Apprehension from enemies

Legends: This *midrashic* explanation explicates the verse in *Exodus 12:1* "This month shall be unto you."

This month shall be unto you. It is written: And I sent before you Moses, Aaron and Miriam *[Micah 6:4]*. This is the meaning of: O send you Your light and Your truth; let them lead me. *[Psalm 43:3] (Exodus Rabbah, Bo, 15:4)*

Notable Quotations

1. Be my judge, O God, and plead my cause against an ungodly nation.
Deliver me from the deceitful and unjust man. (43:1)

2. Why are you cast down, O my soul?
And why you do moan with me?
Hope in God, for I shall yet praise Him,
The salvation of my countenance, and my God. (43:5)

Psalm 44

Theme: A national lament in which the community prays for deliverance from her enemies who have inflicted a humiliating defeat upon it.

Outline: 2-4 God's help in the past
5-9 Nation's trust in God
10-17 Nation's desperate plight
18-23 Israel's faithfulness to God.
24-27 Cry for deliverance

Liturgical Use: None

Practical Use: When feeling distressed

Legends: This is a tale of four hundred boys and girls who were carried off for immoral purposes.

A story is told of four hundred boys and girls who were carried away for immoral purposes. They sensed what they were wanted for and said among themselves, "If we drown in the sea, we shall attain life in the world to come." The eldest among them cited the verse "The Lord said: 'I will bring back from Bashan, I will bring them back to life from the depths of the sea'" [*Psalm 68:23*] and interpreted it as promising: "I will bring back from Bashan," from between the lion's teeth *[bashen*] [*ben shinne]*); "I will bring them back from the depths of the sea"--those who drown in the sea. When the girls heard this, all of them jumped up and leaped into the sea. The boys then drew an inference for themselves, saying: If they, for whom being mounted for the sexual act is natural, prefer death to submission, we, for whom being mounted is unnatural, should all the more prefer death to submission. At that, they also leaped into the sea. Of them, Scripture says, "It is for Your sake that we are slain all day long, that we are regarded as sheep to be slaughtered" *[Psalm*

44:23]. (Talmud Gittin 57b)

Notable Quotations

1. O God, we have heard with our ears, our fathers have told us.
   A work You did in their days, in the days of old. (44:1)

2. In God have we gloried all day,
   And we will give thanks to Your name forever. Selah. (44:9)

3. Arise for your help
   And redeem us for Your mercy's sake. (44:27)

Psalm 45

Theme: This psalm is a wedding song which extols a king and his bride on the occasion of their marriage. As to the identity of the royal bridegroom, various commentators postulated either Solomon or Ahab. Others have asserted that this Psalm refers to King Messiah and the marriage as an allusion to his redemption of Israel.

Outline: 2 Prelude
3-10 Praise of the bridegroom
11-13 Address to the bride
14-16 Description of the bride

Liturgical Use: None

Practical Use: Upon the occasion of someone's marriage.

Legends: This tale speaks of the results of two students who sharpen each other's wit through discussing Jewish law and the use of a proof text in *Psalm 45:5.*

Rabbi Jeremiah said in the name of Rabbi Eleazar: When two disciples of the wise sharpen each other's wit through discussion of halacha, the Holy One gives them success, for Scripture says, "In your majesty [*va-hadarecha*] be successful" (*Psalm 45:5*). Read not *va-hadarecha,* but *va-hadadecha*, your sharpening."

Moreover, they rise to greatness, as is said, they "ride on prosperously" [*Psalm 45:5]*. One might have supposed that this is so even when the discussion in Halacha is not for its own sake. Therefore, the verse goes on to say, "In behalf of truth." One might have supposed that this is so even if the disciple of the wise becomes arrogant. Therefore, the verse goes on to speak of "meekness and righteousness." (*Talmud Shabbat 63a)*

Notable Quotations

1. You are fairer that the children of men.
   Grace is poured on your lips.
   Therefore God has blessed you forever. (45:3)

2. So shall the king desire your beauty.
   For he is your lord and do homage to him. (45:12)

3. I will make your name to be remembered in all generations.
   Therefore, shall the peoples praise you for ever and ever. (45:18)

Psalm 46

Theme: This psalm speaks of a national danger which had been overcome by the mercy of God. It has been asserted that the psalm is speaking of the invasion of the land by Sennacherib's army in the reign of Hezekiah.

Outline: 1-3 Expectation of God's intervention
4-7 God's victory and the new era
8-11 Result of God's intervention

Liturgical Use: None

Practical Use: Disruptive changes in one's life; disaster

Legends: This brief tale is a commentary on the verse in the Book of Esther "Mordecai sat in the King's gate. (2:21)

Rabbi Berechiah said in the name of Rabbi Levi: It is written: "Come, behold the works of God, who has made desolations in the earth. *(Psalm 46:9*) He made servants angry against their master to confer greatness on the righteous, as it says, Bigtan and Teresh were angry--to bestow greatness on Mordecai. He also makes masters angry with their servants, as for instance, to confer greatness on Joseph, as it says, Pharaoh was angry with his servants." [*Genesis 41:10] (Esther Rabbah 6:13)*

Notable Quotations

1. God is our refuge and strength,
   A very present help in trouble. (46:2)

2. Nations were in tumult, kingdoms were moved.
   He uttered His voice, the earth melted. (46:7)

3. The Lord of Hosts is with us.
 The God of Jacob is our high tower. Selah. (46:8)

Psalm 47

Theme: A hymn celebrating God's enthronement as King of all the gods and all the nations. It may refer historically to Assyria's defeat.

Outline: 2-5 Call to the nations
6-7 Praise the king
8-9 God is enthroned

Liturgical Use: The psalm is recited in the synagogue before the sounding of the *shofar* (ram's horn) on Rosh Hashanah, a day when the liturgy dwells on the thought of God's universal kingship and sovereignty.

Legends: This is a tale about the decree that no Jew should remain in all of Rome. It utilizes verse 10 in *Psalm 47* "They among the peoples who volunteer are gathered together, the people of the God of Abraham, for unto God belong the shields of the earth; He is highly exalted."

Once, when our masters Rabbi Eliezer, Rabbi Joshua and Rabban Gamaliel were in Rome, the imperial Senate issued a decree that after thirty days no Jew should remain in the entire Roman world. One senator, who feared Heaven, came to Rabban Gamaliel and disclosed the decree to him. Our masters were greatly distressed, but the man who feared Heaven said to them: Be not distressed. Within the next thirty days the God of the Jews will stand by them. After twenty-five days, he disclosed the decree to his wife, who said: But twenty-five days are already gone. He said: Five days are still left. His wife, even more righteous than he, said: Have you no ring? Suck the poison concealed in it and die. Then the sessions of the Senate will be suspended for thirty days in mourning for you, and the decree will not take effect. He heeded what she had to say, sucked the ring, and died.

When our masters heard of this, they came to his wife to express their sympathy. While there, they said: Alas for the ship that set out to sail without paying the toll. She replied: I understand what you mean. As you live, the ship did not sail until she paid the toll due. Then she went into the bedchamber and brought them a box in which lay the foreskin, wrapped in blood-stained rags. At that, our masters applied to that senator the verse "They among the peoples who volunteer are gathered together, the people of the God of Abraham; for unto God belong the shields of the earth; He is highly exalted" *[Psalm 47:10]*. What is signified by "the shields of the earth?" God said: To Abraham I became a shield of strength. And the proof? Because it is said, "I am your shield" [*Genesis 15:1*]. But to this senator I will become many shields. To Abraham I said, "I will make of you a great nation, and I will bless you, and make your name great" *[Genesis 12:2*], and only after that did he have himself circumcised. But to this senator I made no such promise. What then is signified by "he is highly exalted?" That this one is exalted high above Abraham. *(Deuteronomy Rabbah 2:24; Yalkut, Psalms, parag. 754.)*

Notable Quotations

1. Clap your hands, all you peoples.
   Shout to God with the voice of triumph. (47:2)

2. For God is the King of all the earth.
   Sing praises in skillful song. (47:8)

Psalm 48

Theme: This psalm celebrates the sparing of Jerusalem from the Assyrian invasion. It also celebrates the sovereignty of God who resides in Jerusalem.

Outline: 2-4 God in the midst of Zion
5-9 Defeat of the besiegers
10-15 Meditation upon the event

Liturgical Use: On the second day of the week, the Levites would recite *Psalm 48* in the Temple. *Psalm 48* is the daily Psalm for Monday, recited during morning services each Monday of the year.

Practical Use: When feeling uplifted.

Legends: This is a tale about an incident at the arcade called the Arch of Account, a place where people went to settle accounts.

Rabbi Yochanan said: Outside of Jerusalem there was an arcade called the Arch of Accounts, and when people had accounts to settle, they used to go and settle them under the arch. Thus, it could not happen that a man, while reckoning his account, would be brought to grief, a thing that must not be allowed to occur, because Jerusalem is called "the joy of the whole earth" *[Psalm 48:3].* True, as soon as Jerusalem was destroyed (*charevah*), that joy was darkened *(arevah)* and the gladness of the whole earth was exiled. But when the Holy One rebuilds Jerusalem, He will restore it to all the joy, as is said, God has comforted Zion...Joy and gladness shall be found therein, thanksgiving and the voice of melody" [*Isaiah 51:3]. (Exodus Rabbah 52:5)*

Notable Quotations

1. Great is God, and highly to be praised,

In the city of our God, His holy mountain. (48:2)

2. As is Your name, O God,
So is Your praise unto the ends of the earth.
Your right hand is full of righteousness. (48:11)

Psalm 49

Theme: This is a wisdom psalm reflecting on the momentary nature of wealth and pleasure. One is advised not to envy the rich, for the grave awaits them too.

Outline: 2-5 Exhortatory introduction
6-13 Wealth and death
14-21 Vanity of wealth; triumph of the upright

Liturgical Use: Used as a psalm in a house of mourning.

Practical Use: When confused by success of the wicked, and envious of the rich.

Legends: This tale is a commentary on the verse "Give ear, all you weasel-like inhabitants." ***[Psalm 49:2]*** **[Note: The Hebrew word for world** ***cheled*****, which appears in the Psalm and means world, also means "weasel."]**

"Give ear, all your weasel-like inhabitants." (*Psalm 49:2)* Why does the psalm liken the inhabitants of the world to a weasel? Because, just as a weasel drags things in and stores them without knowing for whom it is storing them, so the inhabitants of the world drag things in and store them without knowing for whom they store them. "He heaps up riches and knows not who shall gather them." *[Psalm 39:7] (Jerusalem Talmud, Shabbat 14:1, 14c)*

Notable Quotations

1. Of those that trust in their wealth,
   And boast themselves in the multitude of their riches,
   No person can by any means redeem his brother,
   Nor give to God a ransom for him. (49:7-8)

2. He sees that wise men die,
   The fool and the brutish together perish,
   And leave their wealth to others. (49:11)

3. When he dies he shall carry nothing away.
   His wealth will not descend after him. (49:18)

Psalm 50

Theme: *Psalm 50* is a prophetic liturgy of divine judgment. In it the psalmist stresses the futility of sacrifice devoid of morality.

Outline: 1-6 Appearance of God
7-15 God's oracle concerning sacrifice
16-23 Superficial legalism

Liturgical Use: None

Practical Use: When feeling thankful to God.

Legends: This is a tale about the daughter of Nehonia who falls into a large pit.

Our masters taught: There is a story about the daughter of Nehonia, the digger of cisterns. When she fell into a large pit that he had dug, people came and reported the accident to Rabbi Hanina ben Dosa. During the first hour, he said to them, "She is all right." during the second hour, he again said, "She is all right." In the third, he said, "She has got out safely." Her father asked her, "My daughter, who saved you?" "A ram, with an aged man leading it, came to my help." "Are you a prophet?" the people asked Rabbi Hanina ben Dosa. He replied, "I am neither a prophet nor the son of a prophet; but I said to myself: It is inconceivable that his own seed should come to grief through the very same beneficent work in which a righteous man is engaged."

Rabbi Abba stated: To be sure, Nehonia's daughter was saved, but Nehonia's son died of thirst, for the Holy One deals strictly with those round about Him, even if they stray by a hairsbreadth, as is said, "Round about Him, it is by a hairsbreadth." *[Psalm 50:3] (Talmud Yevamot 121b)*

Notable Quotations

1. Out of Zion, the perfection of beauty,
   God has shined forth. (50:2)

2. The heavens declare His righteousness.
   For God, He is judge. Selah. (50:6)

3. Whoever offers the sacrifice of thanksgiving honors Me.
   And to him who orders his way aright will I show the salvation of God. (50:23)

Psalm 51

Theme: A lament and prayer of contrition. After an abhorrent crime (which tradition identifies with King David's sin), the psalmist prays for moral purification.

Outline: 1-2 Cry of forgiveness
3-6 Psalmist's confession
7-12 Psalmist's petition for cleansing and renewal
13-17 Psalmist's vow
20-21 Prayer for Temple's restoration

Liturgical Use: None

Practical Use: i. When desiring to repent
ii. Wanting to pray, say psalms, speak to God.

Legends: This tale is a commentary on the verse in *Psalm 51:3* "Have mercy on me, O God, according to Your lovingkindness."

"Have mercy on me, O God, according to Your lovingkindness." With whom may David be compared? With a man who had a wound on his hand and came to a physician. The physician said, "You cannot be treated. The wound is large, but the money you have is little." The man said, "I beg of you, take all the money that I have here, and as for the rest, let it come from you. Have mercy upon me, have compassion upon me." So too, David said to the Holy One, "have mercy upon me, O God, according to Your lovingkindness." You are compassionate, so "according to the multitude of Your compassion blot out my transgressions"; You have already shown me much mercy. David also said, "Make passing great Your mercies, O You that saves them that take refuge in You" *[Psalm 17:7]:* healing comes from You. Because the wound is large, lay on a large poultice for me, as is said, "Wash me thoroughly from my iniquity" *[Psalm 51:4]. (Midrash Tehillim*

51:1] Yalkut Psalms, parag. 764).

Notable Quotations

1. Wash me thoroughly from my iniquity,
   And cleanse me from my sin. (51:4)

2. Create in me a clean heart, O God,
   And renew a steadfast spirit within me. (51:12)

3. Do good in your favor to Zion
   Build the walls of Jerusalem.
   Then will You delight in the sacrifices of righteousness, in burnt offering and whole offering,
   Then will they offer bullocks on Your altar. (51:20-21)

Psalm 52

Theme: This psalm contrasts the destiny of the pagan who relies on his cunning with that of the believer who draws his strength from God.

Outline: 3-7 Denunciation of the oppressor
8-11 Security of the righteous

Liturgical Use: None

Practical Use: Frustration at wickedness of people.

Legends: This tale comments on the verse "Why do you boast yourself of evil, O mighty man?" *[Psalm 52:3*]

"Why do you boast yourself of evil, O mighty man?' [*Psalm 52:3*] David asked Doeg: Is this really might for him who sees his fellow at the edge of a pit to push him into it? Or seeing his fellow on top of a roof, to push him off? Is this might? When a man can truly be called "a mighty man?" When his fellow is about to fall into a pit, and he seizes his hand so that he does not fall in. Or when he sees his fellow fallen into a pit, and he lifts him out of it. *(Midrash Tehillim 52:6)*

Notable Quotations

1. The tongue devises destruction.
   Like a sharp razor, working deceitfully. (52:4)

2. But as for me, I am like a leafy olive-tree in the house of God.
   I trust in the mercy of God forever and ever. (52:10)

Psalm 53

Theme: A revised version of *Psalm 14,* this psalm is a description of the hard lot of Israel in a godless world.

Outline: 1-3 Psalmist's petition for help
4-5 Psalmist's confidence in God
6-7 Psalmist's vow in anticipation of deliverance.

Liturgical Use: None

Practical Use: i. When seeing corruption in world.
ii. Israel, Jews, Judaism pressed, abused, threatened.

Legends: This *midrash* expounds upon the meaning of the word *machalat* in the opening verse of ***Psalm 53.***

The word *Machalat* is to be read in the light of the verse 'whoso finds a wife find a great good. (*Proverbs 18:22)* Endless is the good of a good woman. And even as the good of a good woman is endless, so the evil of an evil woman is endless, as it is said, I find more bitter than death the woman whose heart is snares and nets. (*Ecclesiastes 7:26)* Rabbi Samuel taught, Abigail did more good for David than all the sacrifices in the world. For had David done that deed which he thought to do upon Nabal, then, even if David had brought all the sacrifices in the world, they would not have atoned for him. What she did for him is implied in the verse "To the Eternal God; upon Machalat, even as sacrifices bring about forgiveness, Abigail brought about forgiveness (*mechila)* for David.

Notable Quotations

1. The fool has said in his heart: 'There is no God.
They have dealt corruptly and have done abominable iniquity.
There is none that does good. (53:2)

2. Oh that the salvation of Israel were come out of Zion.
When God turns the captivity of His people,
Let Jacob rejoice, let Israel be glad. (53:7)

Psalm 54

Theme: A lament and supplication of a king for deliverance from his foreign enemies.

Outline: 3-5 Psalmist's peril
6-9 Psalmist's confidence in divine assistance.

Liturgical Use: None

Practical Use: Anxiety from enemies.

Legends: This tale is a comment on the verse in *Exodus* "And he will go up out of the land."

And he will go up out of the land. It does not say 'and we' will go up, but "and he will go up." He spoke, says Rabbi Abba bar Kahana, like a man who means to curse himself, but attaches the curse to others. Another explanation of "And he will go up out of the land" is that Israel will ascend from the lowest degradation, for see what is written: "And he will go up from the land." Similarly, when David said: For our soul is bowed down to the dust; our belly cleaves to the earth" *[Psalm 54:26],* at the same moment he says: Arise for our help and redeem us for Your mercy's sake. *(Psalm 54:27) (Exodus Rabbah 1:9)*

Notable Quotations

1. O God, save me by Your name,
   And right me by Your might. (54:3)

2. Behold, God is my helper.
   The Lord is for me as the upholder of my soul. (54:6)

Psalm 55

Theme: The psalmists lament due to hostility of his fellow citizens. According to tradition, the Psalm relates to Absalom's rebellion, and the "familiar friend" in verse 14 is named as Achitophel in *Ethics of the Fathers 6:3.*

Outline: 2-9 Psalmists cry of distress
10-16 Denunciation of his betrayer
17-22 God the vindicator

Liturgical Use: None

Practical Use: i. Anxiety from enemies
ii. Betrayed or hurt by others
iii. When experiencing great trouble and much distress

Legends: This *midrashic* statement is a commentary on the verse "Oh that I had wings like a dove." *(Psalm 55:7)*

"Oh that I had wings like a dove." (*Psalm 55:7)* Rabbi Azariah said in the name of Rabbi Yudan: All other birds, when tired, rest on a rock or a tree, but the dove, when she gets tired while flying, draws in one of her wings and keeps flying with the other. (*Genesis Rabbah 39:8)*

Notable Quotations:

1. My heart writhes within me.
   And the terrors of death are fallen upon me. (55:5)

2. We took sweet counsel together,
   In the house of God we walked with the multitude. (55:15)

3. Cast your burden upon God and He will sustain you.
   He will never suffer the righteous to be moved. (55:23)

Psalm 56

Theme: A lament of a king who prayers for deliverance from those who slander him.

Outline: 1-2 A cry to God because of enemies
3-4 Trust in the day of fear
5-6 Lament over the activities of his enemies
8-11 His confidence in God's concern
12-13 Payment of his vows

Liturgical Use: None

Practical Use: i. Anxiety from enemies
ii. Need to increase trust in God
iii. Feeling threatened or anxious

Legends: Following is a comment on the assertion that a person is required to bless God for evil, even as he is to bless Him for good.

A man is required to bless God for evil, even as he is to bless God for good, as it is said, "You shall love the Lord your God with all your might *(me'odecha) [Deuteronomy 6:5].* Read rather: "For very measure (*middah)* that may be measured out to you, thank Him. (*modeh)*

What is meant by being bound to bless for the evil in the same way as for the good? Shall I say that, just as for good one says the benediction "Who is good and bestows good," so for evil one should say the benediction "who is good and bestows good?" But we have been taught: For good tidings, one says, "Who is good and bestows good"; for evil tidings, one says, "Blessed be the true Judge." Rava explained: What it really means is that one must accept the evil with gladness. Rav Acha said in the name of Rabbi Levi: Where is the proof? From "I will sing of mercy and justice" *[Psalm*

101:1); be it "mercy", I will sing, or be it "justice," I will sing. Rav Samuel bar Nachmani said: We derive it from "In God I will praise His word: in God I will praise His word. *[Psalm 56:11)* "In God I will praise His word" refers to the measure of good. "In God I will praise His word" refers to the measure of suffering. (*Talmud Berachot 54a, 48b* and *60b)*

Notable Quotations

1. In the day that I am afraid,
   I will put my trust in You. (56:4)

2. In God I will praise His word,
   In God I will praise His word. (56:11)

3. You have delivered my soul from death,
   Have You not delivered my feet from stumbling?
   That I may walk before God in the light of the living. (56:14)

Psalm 57

Theme: Similar in theme to the preceding psalm 56, this psalm is again the lament of a king, harassed by malicious slanderers.

Outline: 2-6 Prayer in persecution
7-12 Steadfastness under trial

Liturgical Use: None

Practical Use: Anxiety from enemies.

Legends: This tale explains R. Mana's statement that a person who speaks slander caused God's Presence to depart from both earth and heaven using as a proof text *Psalm 57: 6:* Be exalted O God above the heavens.

R Mana said: He who speaks slander causes the Presence to depart from the earth below to the heaven above: you may see for yourself that this is so. Consider what David said: "My soul is among lions; I do lie among them that are aflame; even the souls of men, whose teeth are spears and arrows, and their tongue a sharp sword" (*Psalm 57:5)* What follows directly? "Be Thou exalted O God above the heavens" (*Psalm 57:6)* For David said: Master of the universe, what can the Presence do on the earth below? Remove the Presence to the firmament.

Notable Quotations

1. Be gracious to me, God, be gracious to me.
   For in You has my soul taken refuge.
   Yea, in the shadow of Your wings will I take refuge
   Until calamities be overpast. (57:2)

2. They have prepared a net for my steps,

My soul is bowed down,
They have dug a pit for me,
They are fallen into the midst thereof themselves. Selah. (57: 7)

3. I will give thanks to You, O God, among the peoples.
I will sing praises to You among the nations. (57:10)

Psalm 58

Theme: A denunciation of corrupt judges is the theme of *Psalm 58*, in which the psalmist brings a libel suit against his slanderers.

Outline: 2-6 Arraignment of judges
7-9 Vindictive prayers for their destruction
10-11 Vindication of the righteous

Liturgical Use: None

Practical Use: Frustration at wickedness of people.

Legends: This midrash is Rabbi Isaac's commentary on the verse "What is politic for men? Silence, yet speak the truth." [*Psalm 58:2]*

Rabbi Isaac said: What is meant by "What is politic for men" Silence yet speak you the truth" [*Psalm 58:2*]. It means: What is good policy for man in this world? To make himself out as mute. Lest it be thought that a man should remain mute in debate on Torah, the psalm goes on to say, "Yet you speak the truth." (*Talmud Hullin 89a)*

Notable Quotations

1. The wicked are estranged from the womb.
   The speakers of lies go astray as soon as they are born.

2. The righteous will rejoice when he sees the vengeance.
   He shall wash his feet in the blood of the wicked. (58:11)

Psalm 59

Theme: A companion *to Psalm 58*, the Psalmist here passionately beseeches God to destroy his enemies.

Outline: 2-6 God's help invoked
7-8 Description of enemies
9-10 God will intervene
11-14 Fate of the wicked

Liturgical Use: None

Practical Use: Anxiety from enemies. This is one of Rabbi Nachman of Bratzlav's so-called ten healing psalms.

Legends: This legend, a commentary on the verse in *Exodus 7:8* "You shall say unto Aaron: Take the rod" employs the verse in *Psalm 59:7* "They return at evening, they howl like a dog."

"Then you shall say to Aaron: Take your rod." *(Exodus 7:8)* Thus it is written: The rod of your strength God will send out of Zion. *(Psalm 110:2)* God rules over the wicked with a rod. Why? Because they are compared to dogs, as it says: They return at evening, they howl like a dog. [*Psalm 59:7*]. And just as one smites a dog with a stick, so will they be smitten. Hence does it say, 'The rod of your strength.' God said to them: 'Pharaoh is wicked; if he says to you: "Show a wonder for you," smite him with a stick'; as it says: Say unto Aaron, take your rod.

Notable Quotations

1. Deliver me from my enemies, O my God,
   Set me on high from them that rise up against me. (59:2)

2. They return at evening, they howl like a dog,

And go round about the city. (59:7)

3. Consume them in anger, consume them, that they be no more.
And let them know that God rules in Jacob,
Unto the ends of the earth. Selah. (59:14)

Psalm 60

Theme: Similar to *Psalm 44*, this psalm is a national lament in which the community (probably in the person of the king), prays for deliverance from its enemies.

Outline: 3-5 National disaster
6-10 Hope of victory in God's assurance
11-14 God's help essential

Liturgical Use: None

Practical Use: When feeling distressed

Legends: Following is a tale which, using a play on words, comments on the verse "You have compassed this mountain long enough" ***(Deuteronomy 2:3).***

"You have compassed this mountain long enough." [Deuteronomy 2:3] This bears out what Scripture says, "Who will bring me into the fortified city—*matzor*". *[Psalm 60:11*] This refers to Rome. Why does David call it *matzor*? Because it is a city which oppresses (*metzirah*) and diminishes *(mebatzerach*) Israel.

Notable Quotations

1. You have made Your people to see hard things.
   You have made us to drink the wine of staggering. (60:5)

2. Give us help against the adversary.
   For vain is the help of man. (60:13)

Psalm 61

Theme: An individual lament in which the psalmist, away from home, petitions God for restoration.

Outline: 2-4 Appeal for help
5-6 Confidence in God
7-8 Hopes for the King's future
9 His gratitude to God

Liturgical Use: None

Practical Use: When feeling thankful to God.

Legends: This is a *midrash* based on the verse "Let me dwell in Your tent forever." *(Psalm 61:5)*

David said: "Let me dwell in Your tent forever" *[Psalm 61:5]*. Could David have believed that he would live forever? No. What David asked the Holy One was: May it be the will of Your Presence that my songs and paeans of praise be uttered in synagogues and houses of study forever. *(Jerusalem Talmud Berachot 2:1; 4a)*

Notable Quotations

1. From the end of the earth will I call to You, when my heart faints.
   Lead me to a rock that is too high for me. (61:3)

2. So I will sing praise to Your name forever,
   That I may daily perform my vows. (61:9)

Psalm 62

Theme: A psalm of trust, in which the psalmist turns to God as the only safe refuge from the storm raging round about him.

Outline: 1-2 Psalmist's soul in quietude before God
3-4 Indignant lamentation directed to his opponents
5-7 Psalmist's silent confidence in God
8-12 Grounds for Psalmist's confidence

Liturgical Use: None

Practical Use: i. Anxious concern about livelihood
ii. Need to increase trust in God.

Legends: This *midrash* attempts to prove the point that there is no set time for prayer.

"As for me, let my prayer be unto You, O God, in an acceptable time." For everything the Holy Blessed One, set a time and a season, as is said, "There is a time for every experience, including the doom" [*Ecclesiastes 8:6)* --except for prayer. Whenever a man prays, he is answered. Why is no time set for prayer? Were a man to know the time when, if he prays, he will be answered, he would leave off other times and pray only then. Accordingly, the Holy Blessed One, said: For this reason, I do not let you know when you will be answered, so that you will be willing to always pray, as is said, "Put your trust in Him at all times*" [Psalm 62:9]. (Aggadat Bereshit 77)*

Notable Quotations

1. God only is my rock and my salvation,
   My high tower, I shall not be greatly moved. (62:3)

2. Men of low degree are vanity, and men of high degree are a lie.
If they be laid in the balances, they are together lighter than vanity. (62:10)

3. God has spoken once,
Twice have I heard this:
That strength belongs to God. (62:12)

Psalm 63

Theme: A king's prayer for the angelic vision in the heavenly sanctuary. This psalm is a psalm of trust. Some Bible critics assert that the author of this psalm is a Levite in exile who is desirous to again participate in the Temple service in Jerusalem.

Outline: 2-5 Yearning for the sanctuary
6-8 Remembrance of past mercies
9-12 Psalmist's fate and his persecutors

Liturgical Use: None

Practical Use: When in the synagogue

Legends: This brief tale is a commentary on the verse "By His sword with all flesh" ***(Isaiah 66:16)***

The Egyptians said: "With what shall we destroy the Israelites. Shall we destroy them with fire? But it has already been said: "For by fire will God contend." *(Isaiah 66:16*) Shall we destroy them with the sword? But it is already written, "And by His sword with all flesh" *(Isaiah 66:16)*. Let us then destroy them with water, since God has already sworn that He will not again bring a flood on the world, as it is written, "For this is as the waters of Noah unto Me." (*Isaiah 54:9) (Song of Songs Rabbah 2:15, parag. 1)*

Notable Quotations

1. O God, You are my God, earnestly will I seek You.
   My soul thirsts for You, my flesh longs for You,
   In a dry and weary land, where there is no water. (63:2)

2. I will bless You as long as I live.
   In Your name will I lift up my hands. (63:5)

3. My soul cleaves to You.
   Your right hand holds me fast. (63:9)

Psalm 64

Theme: The psalmist, overwhelmed by fear of the enemies, laments unto God and prays for protection.

Outline: 2-7 Prayer for protection
8-11 God will thwart the schemers

Liturgical Use: None

Practical Use: When in a situation of danger and in need of God's protection.

Legends: This tale attempts to explain the meaning of "Hear my voice, God, when I plead." (*Psalm 64:1)*

It is written in the *Book of Amos 3:7*: "Indeed, my Lord God does nothing without having revealed His purpose to His servants. God informed David what to do to Daniel and to those who could go upward to make war. And the sons of Korach say: "They made Your sanctuary go up in flames."

Notable Quotations:

1. Hear my voice, O God, in my complaint.
   Preserve my life from the terror of the enemy. (64:2)

2. The righteous shall be glad in the Lord and shall take refuge in Him.
   And all the upright in heart shall glory. (64:11)

Psalm 65

Theme: A hymn of public thanksgiving for an abundant harvest. The Bible commentator Ibn Ezra held the opinion that the psalm was composed by a chorister for the occasion of the building of the Jerusalem Temple

Outline: 2-5 Praise to God in the Temple
6-9 God's awe-inspiring deeds
10-14 Thanksgiving for the harvest

Liturgical Use: None

Practical Use: i. In the synagogue
ii. Feeling of thankfulness to God

Legends: This *midrash is* a commentary on the verse "I will give the rain of your land in its season, the former rain (*yoreh*) and the latter rain *(malkosh) [Deuteronomy 11:14]*

"I will give the rain of your land in its season, the former rain *(yoreh*) and the latter rain *(malkosh) [Deuteronomy 11:14].* Our masters taught: The former rain is called *yoreh* because it instructs (*yoreh*) people to plaster their roofs, to gather in their produce, and to attend to all their other needs for the winter. Another explanation: It is called *yoreh* because it saturates the soil and waters it to its nethermost depths: "Saturating *(raveh)* her furrows, leveling her rides, You make her soft with showers; You bless the growth thereof." [*Psalm 65:11] (Talmud Taanit 6a)*

Notable Quotations

1. Happy is the person who You choose and bring near.
   That he may dwell in Your courts.
   May we be satisfied with the goodness of Your house,

The holy place of Your Temple. (65:5)

2. The meadows are clothed with flocks.
The valleys also are covered over with corn.
They shout for joy, yea, they sing. (65:14)

Psalm 66

Theme: This psalm has two distinct parts: verses 1-12 being a national song of thanksgiving, and verses 13-20 being a narrative of the payment of the vow of an individual.

Outline: 1-4 Earth summoned to praise God
5-7 God's hand in Israel's history.
8-12 A renewed summons to the nations
13-20 Payment of the vow of an individual

Liturgical Use: None

Practical Use: Feeling of thankfulness to God.

Legends: This legend is in answer to a question posed to Rabbi Joshua ben Korach concerning when both heathens and Jews rejoice at the same time.

A certain heathen inquired of Rabbi Joshua ben Korcha saying to him: You have your festivals, and we have ours. When you are rejoicing, we are not, and when we are rejoicing, you are not. When do both you and we rejoice? When rain comes down. And what is the proof? The verse "The meadows are clothed with flocks; the valleys also are covered with corn; they shout for joy, yea, they sing." *[Psalm 65:14).* And what follows directly? "Shout to God, all the earth" *[Psalm 66:1]* --not just priests, Levites, or lay Israelites, but all the earth. (*Genesis Rabbah 13:6)*

Notable Quotations

1. Sing praises unto the glory of His name.
   Make His praise glorious. (66:2)

2. Bless our God, you peoples,

And make the voice of His praise to be heard. (66:8)

3. Blessed be God,
Who has not turned away my prayer, nor His mercy from me. (66:13)

Psalm 67

Theme: A harvest song sung during the Feast of Tabernacles.

Outline: 2-3 Recognition of God through Israel
4-5 May all humanity acknowledge God
6-8 Effect of Allegiance to God

Liturgical Use: None

Practical Use: When feeling thankful for your bounty

Legends: This *midrash* is an exposition on the verse that is part of the so-called Priestly blessing "And be gracious unto you." *[Numbers 6:25]*

"And be gracious unto you" accords with the text "God be gracious unto us and bless us; may God cause His face to shine toward us. Selah. *[Psalm 67:2] (Numbers Rabbah: 11:6)*

Notable Quotations

1. God be gracious to us and bless us.
May God cause His face to shine toward us. Selah. (67:2)

2. Let the nations be glad and sing for joy.
For You will judge the peoples with equity,
And lead the nations upon earth. Selah. (67:5)

8. May God bless us.
And let all the ends of the earth fear God. (67:8)

Psalm 68

Theme: Israel's triumphant ode, a review of God's victories over the centuries.

Outline: 2-7 Advent of God and its effects
8-19 The past reviewed
20-24 God will continue to deliver in the future
25-28 Procession to the Temple
29-32 Appeal to God to subdue all peoples
33-36 Let all nations join in God's praise

Liturgical Use: None

Practical Use: i. Anxious concern about livelihood
ii. When single, hoping to find a soul mate

Legends: This tale illustrates using biblical verses Rabbi Yochanan's assertion that whenever God's power is mentioned in the Bible, you also find condescension mentioned as well.

Rabbi Yochanan said: Whenever you find the power of the Holy Blessed One mentioned in Scripture, you also find His condescension mentioned, a fact that is stated in the *Five Books*, repeated in the Prophets, and reasserted in the Writings. In the *Five Books* it is written, "For the Lord your God, He is God of gods" *[Deuteronomy 10:17*), and directly after that, "He does execute justice for the fatherless and the widow" *[Deuteronomy 10:18*). It is repeated in the Prophets: "For thus says the high and lofty one, I dwell in the high and lofty place" *[Isaiah 57:15]*, and directly after that, "With him also that is of a contrite and humble spirit" [*Isaiah 57:15*]. And reasserted in the Writings: "Extol Him that rides on the skies, whose name is the Lord" *[Psalm 68:5*].

Notable Quotations

1. A father of the fatherless, and a judge of the widows,
   Is God in His holy habitation. (68:6)

2. Blessed be God, day by day God bears our burden,
   Even the God who is our salvation. Selah. (68:20)

3. Ascribe strength to God.
   God's majesty is over Israel,
   And God's strength is in the skies. (68:35)

Psalm 69

Theme: A lament of an individual who prays for deliverance from his enemies. According to some modern Bible scholars, the author of this psalm is the Prophet Jeremiah.

Outline: 2-7 Appeal for help
8-13 He suffers in God's cause
14-19 Prayer for deliverance
20-22 His sufferings retold
30-37 Deliverance awaits him and Israel

Liturgical Use: Verse 14 "As for me, let my prayer be unto You, O Lord, in an acceptable time; O God, in the abundance of Your mercy, answer me with the truth of Your salvation" provide the closing words of the opening prayer of the daily service called *Ma Tovu.*

Practical Use: Great troubles and distress

Legends: This *midrashic* explanation by Rabbi Yose utilizes the verse "As for me, let my prayer be unto You O God in an acceptable time." [*Psalm 69:14]*

Quoting "As for me, let my prayer be unto You O God, in an acceptable time" *[Psalm 69:14],* Rabbi Yose bar Halafta said: This means that there are acceptable times for prayer and that David prayed to the Holy Blessed One: Whenever I pray before You, may it be an acceptable time. *(Jerusalem Talmud Makkot 2:6; 31d)*

Notable Quotations

1. I am weary with my crying, my throat is dried,
   My eyes fail while I wait for God. (69:4)

2. But as for me, let my prayer be unto You, O God, in an acceptable time.
O God, in the abundance of Your mercy,
Answer me with the truth of Your salvation. (69:14)

3. Hide not Your face from my servant.
For I am in distress; answer me speedily. (69:18)

Psalm 70

Theme: *Psalm 70* is the lament of an old man who prays for deliverance from personal enemies. The psalm is a reproduction of *Psalm 40:14-18.*

Outline: 2-6 Plea for help

Liturgical Use: None

Practical Use: When in need of help and in obvious distress.

Legends: This tale is a commentary on the verse "Behold, this I have found, says Kohelet." ***[Ecclesiastes 7:27)***

"Behold, this I have found, says (*amerah*) Kohelet." *[Ecclesiastes 7:27*]. The verb *amerah* is feminine. Elsewhere, it is written, "Says (*amar*) Kohelet" [*Ecclesiastes 1;2*]. The verb *amar* is masculine. Rabbi Jeremiah explained: The two forms of the verb allude to the holy spirit, which sometimes speaks using a masculine form and at other times a feminine form. Thus one verse reads, "You are my help *(ezri*, masculine) and my deliverer" [*Psalm 70:6*], while another verse reads, "You are my help (*ezrati*, feminine) and my deliverer" [*Psalm 40:18*] One verse reads, "How beautiful upon the mountains are the feet of the messenger of good tidings (*mevasser*, masculine) *[Isaiah 52:7],* while another verse reads, "O you that tells good tidings (*mevasseret,* feminine) to Zion, get you up into the high mountain." [*Isaiah 40:9] (Ecclesiastes Rabbah 7:27, parag. 1; Yalkut, Ecclesiastes, parag. 977)*

Notable Quotations

1. Let all those that seek You rejoice and be glad in You.
   And let such as love Your salvation say continually: 'Let God be magnified.' (70:5)

2. But I am poor and needy.
O God, make haste unto me.
You are my help and my deliverer.
O God do not delay. (70:6)

Psalm 71

Theme: A prayer offered by an old man who suffers many trials and who petitions God for deliverance.

Outline: 1-3 Trust in God
4-13 Appeal for deliverance
14-16 His steadfast hope in God

Liturgical Use: None

Practical Use: i. Anxiety from enemies
ii. Beset by old age

Legends: This tale answers the question: What is it that preserves both heavenly and earthly things?

Rav Abba commented in the name of Rav Berechiah: What is it that preserves the heavenly and earthly things? The charitable deeds which they perform with the hand. Hence it is written, Your charity also, O God, which reaches to the high heaven. *[Psalm 71:19] (Leviticus Rabbah 26:8)*

Notable Quotations

1. In you, O God, I have taken refuge,
Let me never be ashamed. (71:1)

2. My mouth shall be filled with Your praise,
And with Your glory all day. (71:8)

3. My lips shall greatly rejoice when I sing praises unto You.
And my soul, which You have redeemed. (71:23)

Psalm 72

Theme: A prayer for God's blessing on the king. The psalm portrays an ideal monarch and an ideal rule.

Outline: 1-4 Prayer and wishes for a reign of righteousness and peace

5-7 His ending reign
8-11 Extent of his dominion
12-14 Reward of his righteousness
15 Reward from the hearts of the poor
16-17 Resultant rich harvests and enduring fame

Liturgical Use: In the daily evening service after the prayer called the Shema, we praise God as Creator and Sovereign over all creation. Verses 18-19: "Blessed be the Lord God, the God of Israel, who does wondrous things. And blessed be God's glorious name forever. And let the whole earth be filled with God's glory, Amen and Amen" appear in this prayer of praise to God.

Practical Use: When feeling desirous of praising God's sovereignty

Legends: This tale is about the gifts that Jacob gave to Esau in biblical times.

An unlearned man said to Rabbi Hoshaia, "If I tell you a good thing, will you repeat it in public in my name?" Rabbi Hoshaia said: 'What is it?" "All those gifts," he replied, "that our father Jacob gave to Esau, the nations of the world are going to give back to the king Messiah in the time to come." "What proof do you have?" The verse 'The kings of Tarshish and of the isles shall return tribute' [*Psalm 72:10]*. Scripture does not say, 'Shall bring,' but 'Shall return.'" "By your life," Rabbi Hoshaia exclaimed, "you said a good thing, and I will teach it in your name." *(Genesis Rabbah 78:12)*

Notable Quotations

1. Let the mountains bear peace to the people,
And the hills, through righteousness. (72:3)

2. In his days let the righteous flourish,
And abundance of peace, till the moon be no more. (72:7)

3. Blessed be the Lord God, the God of Israel,
Who only does wondrous things.
And blessed be God's glorious name forever.
And let the whole earth be filled with His glory.
Amen and amen. (72:18-19)

Psalm 73

Theme: *Psalm 73* begins Book III of the Book of Psalms. It is a wisdom psalm in which the psalmist reflects on the justice of God. Like the *Book of Job*, the psalmist wonders how one can reconcile God's justice with the governmental inequities in the world.

Outline: 1-2 Introductory statement
3-9 Prosperity of the wicked
10-11 Evil effects of the wicked upon the people
12-14 The Psalmists reflection
18-20 Fate of the wicked
23-26 Psalmist's trust in God returns

Liturgical Use: None

Practical Use: i. In the synagogue
ii. Confused by success of the wicked

Legends: This tale is a commentary on the verse "Death and life are in the hand of the tongue" [*Proverbs 18:21]*

In considering the verse "Death and life are in the hand of the tongue" *[Proverbs 18:21],* Rabbi Hama son of Rav Hanina asked: Is it conceivable for the tongue to have a hand? No, but what the verse really means is that the tongue can be as murderous as the hand. One might have thought that, just as the hand can kill only what is near it, so the tongue could kill only what is near it. Therefore Scripture says, "Their tongue is an arrow shot out" *[Jeremiah 9:7].* One might assume that, just as an arrow kills only up to a distance of forty or at most fifty cubits, so the tongue could kill only up to a distance of forty at most fifty cubits. Therefore Scripture says, "They have set their mouths against the heavens, while their tongues range over the earth." *[Psalm 73:9]. (Talmud Arachin 15b)*

Notable Quotations

1. I was envious at the arrogant,
When I saw the prosperity of the wicked. (73:3)

2. You will guide me with Your counsel,
And afterward receive me with glory. (73:24)

3 But, as for me, the nearness of God is my God.
I have made the Lord God my refuge,
That I may tell of all Your works. (73:28)

Psalm 74

Theme: A national lament. In this lament many Bible commentators find a description of the destruction of the Temple by the Babylonians in 586 B.C.E.

Outline: 1-3 Appeal to God
4-9 Chaos in the Temple
10-11 Appeal to God renewed
12-17 Might of God
18-23 Concluding prayer

Liturgical Use: None

Practical Use: Israel, Jews, Judaism, pressed, abused, threatened

Legends: This is tale about 300 mules sent by King Nebuchadnezzar which mysteriously vanished at the Jerusalem gate.

Rava said: Nebuchadnezzar sent Nebuzaradan three hundred mules laden with iron axes so sharp that they could crack iron, and all of them vanished when a single gate of Jerusalem opened and sucked them in, as is said, "And now a single gate opened upon the axes and pikes they battled with" *[Psalm 74:6]*. Nebuzaradan wanted to retreat, saying to himself: I fear that what happened to Sennacherib will happen to me. But a divine voice went forth: "O leaper, and son of a leaper, Nebuzaradan, leap. The time for the Temple to be destroyed, and for the Sanctuary to be consumed by fire has come." He had only one ax left. Leaping up, he struck the gate with the ax's wooden shaft and the gate opened wide, as is said, "A man became famous for lifting up the part of an ax that is wrought from the sturdy portion of a tree" *[Psalm 74:5]*. Nebuzaradan leaped in and kept hewing down Jews, until he reached the Sanctuary. When he tried to set it on fire, the Sanctuary lifted itself up. But from heaven it was trod upon so hard that it was forced down: 'As in a winepress God trod upon the most sacred part of fair Judah" *[Lamentations 1:15*]. Nebuzaradan was elated. But a divine voice came forth and proclaimed, "A people already slain you slew, a Sanctuary already consumed by fire you set on fire, flour already ground you ground. (*Talmud Sanhedrin 96b)*

Notable Quotations

1. How long, O God, shall the adversary reproach?
   Shall the enemy blaspheme Your name forever? (74:10)

2. Yours is the day, Yours also the night.
   You have established luminary and sun. (74:16)

3. Arise, O God, plead Your own cause.
   Remember Your reproach all the day at the hand of the base man. (74:22)

Psalm 75

Theme: A thanksgiving psalm for delivery from peril and danger. Some Bible commentators date the Psalm after the invasion of Sennacherib, King of Assyria.

Outline: 1 Theme of thanksgiving
2-5 Divine warning against foes
6-8 God, the supreme arbiter of human destiny
9-10 A vow of praise

Liturgical Use: None

Practical Use: When feeling thankful

Legends: This tale comments on the verse "For God is a judge; He puts down one and lifts up another." [*Psalm 75:8]*

"For God is judge. He puts down one, and lifts up another" *[Psalm 75:8*] To what may this world be compared? To a garden's waterwheel. Its clay dippers below come up full, and those above go down empty. So, too, not everyone who is rich today will be rich tomorrow, and not everyone who is poor today will be poor tomorrow, for the world is a wheel. *(Exodus Rabbah 31:3)*

Notable Quotations

1. We give thanks to You, O God
   We give thanks, and Your name is near.
   Men tell of Your wondrous works. (75:2)

2. For God is judge.
   He puts down one and lifts up another. (75:8)

3. All the horns of the wicked also will I cut off.

But the horns of the righteous shall be lifted up. (75:11)

Psalm 76

Theme: The defeat of Israel's enemy is a glorification of the Name of God. This psalm resembles psalms 46 and 48, which celebrate God's victory over the nations.

Outline: 2-4 God's victory in Zion
5-7 The enemy's collapse
11-13 Surely the wrath of man shall praise You.

Liturgical Use: None

Practical Use: When desirous of praising God.

Legends: This tale is a commentary on the verse "The stouthearted are bereft of sense...and none of the men of might could lift a hand" [*Psalm 76:6]*

"Send you men" [*Numbers 13:2].* These words are to be considered in the light of what Scripture says elsewhere: "The stouthearted are bereft of sense...and none of the men of might could lift a hand" *[Psalm 76:6].* The words "bereft of sense" and "none could lift a hand" apply to Moses and Aaron, who sent out the scouts. When these came and spoke slander about the land, no one knew what to do--even Moses and Aaron could not, so to speak, lift a hand.

"Moses sent them to scout the land of Canaan and said to them: 'Get you up here into the southland and go up into the mountains'" *[Numbers 13:17*]. Such is the way of traders--they show the inferior wares first, and then display the best. *(Numbers Rabbah 16:2 and 16:12; Yalkut, Shelach, parag. 742)*

Notable Quotations

1. Glorious are You and excellent,

Coming down from the mountains of prey. (76:5)

2. You caused sentence to be heard from heaven.
The earth was afraid and was still. (76:9)

Psalm 77

Theme: A lamentation poem, in which the psalmist gives voice to a woeful situation. Verses 14-20 are a hymn of praise to God for His glorious deeds of the past.

Outline: 1-3 I will cry, and God will answer
4-9 Musings on the Divine mercies in the past
10-15 God's power and mercy manifested in His dealings with Israel
16-19 God's power over nature.
20 Conclusion

Liturgical Use: None

Practical Use: When anxious, suffering, or afflicted. This is one of Rabbi Nachman of Breslov's ten healing psalms.

Legends: This tale details the cause of thunder.

What causes thunder? Samuel said: Clouds that rub against each other while whirling about, as Scripture says, "The voice of Your thunder was in the whirlwind; the lightning lighted up the world, the earth trembled and shook" *[Psalm 77:19].* The sages, however, said: Clouds that pour water into each other. Rabbi Acha bar Jacob said: A powerful lightning that strikes clouds and breaks off chunks of ice. Rav Ashi said: There are hollows in the clouds, and when a blast of wind comes and blows through these hollows, it makes a sound like wind blowing across the opening of a cask. Rav Acha bar Jacob's explanation is the most likely, for when lightning flashes, the clouds rumble, and then rain begins to fall. (*Talmud Berachot 59a)*

Notable Quotations

1. I will raise my voice to God and cry.
   I will lift up my voice to God so that He may listen to me. (77:2)

2. You hold fast the lids of my eyes.
   I am troubled and am unable to speak. (77:5)

3. O God, Your way is the way of holiness.
   Who is a great Lord like you? (77:14)

Psalm 78

Theme: A wisdom psalm, whose purpose is to instruct the present from the experiences of the past. Bible commentators have asserted that it was composed prior to the Babylonian captivity.

Outline: 1-8 Psalmist recalls the past as a means of teaching the future

9-31 Ephraim's disobedience despite Divine mercy
32-39 Superficial repentance
40-56 The more God showed His Mercy, the more the people rebelled.
57-64 Divine leadings during the period of the Judges
65-72 Choice of Zion and of David

Liturgical Use: None

Practical Use: When having an anxiety attack.

Legends: This tale explains the verse "The angel of God, who had been going ahead of the Israelite host, now moved and followed behind them" ***[Exodus 14:19].***

"The angel of God, who had been going ahead of the Israelite host, now moved and followed behind them" [*Exodus 14:19].* To understand what the angel of God did, consider the parable of a man walking on the road and making his son walk in front of him. When brigands attempting to capture the son came up in front, the father pulled his son from in front of him and put him behind. When a wolf came up behind, the father pulled his son from behind and put him in front. When brigands came up in front while a wolf came up behind, he took the son into his arms. When the son began to suffer from the heat, the father spread his cloak over him. When he was hungry, he fed him. When he was thirsty, he gave him to drink. So too did the Holy One: When the sea was in front of Israel and the Egyptians behind, God took them into His arms--"taking them upon His arms" *[Hosea 11:3*]. When they began to suffer from the sun, He spread His garment over them, as is said, "he spread a cloud for a screen" *[Psalm 105:39].* When they were hungry, God fed them: "Behold, I will cause to rain bread from heaven for you" *[Exodus 16:4*]. When they were thirsty, He gave them water to drink: "God brought forth streams from a rock" *[Psalm 78:16]. (Mechilta Beshallach, Vayechi 5; Tanchuma Beshallach, parag. 10)*

Notable Quotations

1. I will open my mouth with a parable.
   I will utter dark sayings concerning days of old. (78:2)

2. They remembered that God was their Rock
   And the Most High God was their Redeemer. (78:35)

3. He shepherded them according to the integrity of his heart,
And led them by the skillfulness of his hands. (78:72)

Psalm 79

Theme: A national lament of the Jewish people as a result of the foreign invasion of Jerusalem.

Outline: 1-4 Sufferings endured by Psalmist and his people
5-8 Prayer for help
9-12 Prayer for deliverance
13 Vow of thanksgiving

Liturgical Use: In the *Tachanun* supplicatory prayers recited daily in the morning, the verse "Help us O God, of our salvation, for the sake of the glory of Your name; and deliver us, and forgive our sins, for Your name's sake" appears toward the end.

Practical Use: When feeling anxious or threatened.

Legends: This tale is a comment on the opening verse of *Psalm 79:* "A Psalm of Asaph, O God, the heathen are come into Your inheritance."

" A Psalm of Asaph, O God, the heathen are come into Your inheritance" *[Psalm 79:1].* Should not Scripture have used a phrase such as "weeping of Asaph," "lament of Asaph," "dirge of Asaph?" Why does it say, "A Psalm of Asaph?" The use of the world "psalm" may be accounted for by the parable of a king who made a bridal bower for his son, which he plastered, paneled, and painted. But his son entered upon an evil course of living. So the king came up into the bower and tore the curtains and broke the rods. Then the son's tutor took a reed pipe and played on it. He was asked, "The king has just now overthrown his son's bower, and you sit here playing a tune?" The tutor replied, "I play a tune because the king overthrew his son's bower but did not pour out his wrath upon his son." So, too, when it was said to Asaph, "The Holy One has just destroyed both Temple Hall and Sanctuary, and you sit here singing a psalm?" He replied: "I sing because the Holy One poured out His wrath upon sticks and stones but did not pour out His wrath upon Israel." (*Lamentations Rabbah 4:11, parag. 14)*

Notable Quotations

1. They had shed blood like water,
   Round about Jerusalem, with none to bury them. (79:3)

2. Help us O God of our salvation, for the sake of the glory of Your name.
   And deliver us, and forgive our sins, for Your name's sake. (79:9)

3. We are Your people and the flock of Your pasture.
   We will offer thanks to Your forever,
   We will speak of your praise to all generations. (79:13)

Psalm 80

Theme: A prayer offered in time of national straits. This psalm likely belongs to the last days of the Northern Kingdom.

Outline: 2-4 Cry of the people for help
5-8 People's desperate plight
9-14 Contrast between present and past
15-20 Renewal of prayer

Liturgical Use: None

Practical Use: When experiencing anxiety

Legends: This tale is based on the verse "You did pluck up a vine out of Egypt" ***[Psalm 80:9)***

"You did pluck up a vine out of Egypt" [*Psalm 80:9*]. Rabbi Tanchuma bar Abba asked: "Why is Israel compared to a vine? Consider what owners of a vine, seeking to improve it, do. They pluck it from its place and replant it elsewhere, and there it flourishes. So, too, when the Holy One sought to make Israel known throughout the world, what did He do? He plucked them out of Egypt and brought them into the wilderness, and there they began to thrive; there they received the Torah, and their name went forth throughout the world. *(Exodus Rabbah 44:1)*

Notable Quotations

1. O God, restore us.
   Cause Your face to shine, and we shall be saved. (80:4)

2. O Lord, God of Hosts,
   How long will you be angry against the prayer of Your people? (80:5)

Psalm 81

Theme: A hymn composed either for the festival of Sukkot or the festival of Passover.

Outline: 2-6 Summons to observe the festival
7-8 God's redemptive acts
12-13 Israel's disloyalty
14-17 God's appeal to Israel

Liturgical Use: On the fifth day of the week (Thursday) the Levites would recite this psalm in the Temple. Today *Psalm 81* is used as the daily psalm each week for Thursday.

Practical Use: When desirous of getting closer to God.

Legends: Following is a tale taught by Rabbi Yochanan ben Nuri as to who might be defined as an idolater.

We have been taught that the sages said in the name of Rabbi Yochanan ben Nuri: You are to regard as an idolater the man who in his anger tears his garments, in his anger smashes his vessels, in his anger scatters his money, because such is the craftiness of the impulse to evil. One day, the impulse says to him, "Do this"; the next day, "Do that"; until finally it says, "Go worship an idol," and the man goes and worships it. Rabbi Avin said: And the proof? The verse "There shall be no strange god in you; then you shall not worship an alien god" [*Psalm 81:10*]. What strange god is there within a man's body? You must admit, it is the impulse to evil. (*Talmud Shabbat 105b; Niddah 13b)*

Notable Quotations

1. Sing with joy to God, our strength.

Shout with happiness to the God of Jacob. (81:1)

2. Hear this warning, My people,
   Israel, if you would only listen to Me. (81:9)

3. Blow the horn at the new moon,
   At the full moon for the festive day. (81:4)

4. You would I feed with the fat of wheat,
   And with honey out of the rock would I satisfy you. (81:17)

Psalm 82

Theme: A prophetic liturgy of God's judgment on pagan gods.

Outline: 1-4 Arraignment of the unjust judges
5-7 Their sentence
8 Psalmist's appeal to God

Liturgical Use: On the third day (i.e., Wednesday) of the week the Levites would recite Psalm 82 in the Temple. Today Psalm 82 is recited each Wednesday as the Psalm of the Day.

Practical Use: When feeling the need for a just decision.

Legends: The following tale uses the first verse of *Psalm 82* to prove that the Holy Blessed One is found in a house of prayer.

Ravin bar Rav Adda said in the name of Rabbi Isaac: What is the proof that the Holy Blessed One is found in a house of prayer? The verse "God stands in the congregation of God" *[Psalm 82:1]* And what is the proof that when ten people pray together, the Presence is with them? The verse "God stands in the congregation of God." *(Talmud Berachot 6b)*

Notable Quotations

1. How long will your pervert justice?
   And respect the persons of the wicked. Selah. (82:2)

2. Rescue the poor and needy,
   Deliver them out of the hand of the wicked. (82:4)

3. Arise, God, and judge the earth,
   For You shall possess all the nations. (82:8)

Psalm 83

Theme: A national lament in which the psalmist prays on behalf of the nation for deliverance from the evil foe.

Outline: 2-6 Cry for help in danger
7-9 Alliance against Israel
10-19 Prayer for their overthrow

Liturgical Use: None

Practical Use: Anxiety from enemies

Legends: This brief tale compares Israel to a heap of wheat and the heathens to straw, based on a verse in the *Book of Psalms*.

"Your belly is like a heap of wheat." *(Song of Songs 7:3*) Israel has been compared to a heap of wheat. As the measures of wheat are counted when carried into the barn, so, said the Holy Blessed One, shall Israel be numbered on all occasions. Therefore, it is written, 'Your belly is like a heap of wheat.' The straw and stubble, however, are neither numbered nor measured. So are the heathens likened unto stubble and straw, as it is said, Make them...as stubble before the wind [Psalm 83:14], and the house of Esau shall be for stubble. *[Obadiah 1:18]* Why? Because the Holy Blessed One derives no pleasure from them, as it is said, All the nations are as nothing before Him. *[Isaiah 40:17] (Numbers Rabbah 1:4)*

Notable Quotations

1. They hold crafty chat against Your people,
   And take counsel against Your treasured ones. (83:4)

2. My God, make them like the whirling dust,
   As stubble before the wind. (83:14)

Psalm 84

Theme: A combination of themes, including elements of a Pilgrim song on the occasion of a pilgrimage to the Jerusalem Temple as well as a song of Zion. *Psalm 84* begins the Korach collection of Psalms.

Outline: 1-4 Psalmist's delight in the Temple
5-8 Blessing and strength of God
9-13 Prayer in the Temple

Liturgical Use: None

Practical Use: i. In the synagogue
ii. Need to increase your trust in God

Legends: This tale uses the verse "Happy are they that dwell in Your house now, they will be praising You forever" as its proof text.

Rabbi Joshua ben Levi said: He who utters song in praise of God in this world will merit uttering it in the world to come, as is said, "Happy are they that dwell in Your house now, they will be praising You forever. Selah." [*Psalm 84:5]*

Rabbi Hiyya bar Abba said in the name of Rabbi Yochanan: All the prophets are destined to utter song with one voice, as is said, "Hark, Your watchmen raise their voices; as one they shout for joy" *[Isaiah 52:8]*

Notable Quotations

1. My soul yearns and pines for God's courts,
   My heart and body sing for joy to the living God. (84:3)

2. Happy are they that dwell in Your house,

They are ever praising You. Selah. (84:5)

3. O Lord of Hosts,
Happy is the person that trusts in You. (84:13)

Psalm 85

Theme: Prayer for God's mercy upon the nations and for the returned exiles.

Outline: 1-3 Divine mercies already experienced
4-7 Prayer that God may entirely restore them
8-13 God's response and assurance for the future

Liturgical Use: None

Practical Use: When in need of forgiveness

Legends: This tale enumerates the seven qualities that minister before the throne of glory.

Seven qualities minister before the throne of glory: faithfulness, righteousness, justice, lovingkindness, compassion, truth, and peace, as is said, "I will betroth you to Me in righteousness and in justice, in lovingkindness and in compassion, and I will betroth you to Me in faithfulness, and you shall know God" *[Hosea 2:21*]; and "mercy and truth are met together; righteousness and peace have kissed each other' [*Psalm 85:11] (Avot de Rabbi Natan, 37)*

Notable Quotations

1. God, you have been favorable to Your land,
   You have turned the captivity of Jacob. (85:2)

2. Will You forever be angry with us?
   Will you extend Your anger to all generations? (85:6)

3. Righteousness shall go before Him,
   And shall make His footsteps a way. (85:14)

Psalm 86

Theme: A meditation to be used by any person in time of difficulty, this psalm is a compilation of quotations from the Psalter and other parts of the Bible

Outline: 1-5 Plea for a hearing
6-10 Confident of a response
11-13 Prayer for guidance
14-17 Prayer for protection

Liturgical Use: Verse 8 "There is none like unto You, among the gods, O Lord, and there are no works like Yours" was chosen as the opening verse for the Service for taking out the Torah on the Sabbaths and Festivals.

Practical Use: Great troubles and distress.

Legends: This tale is a commentary on "For You are great and do wondrous things."

"For you are great and do wondrous things" *[Psalm 86:10]*. Rabbi Tanchum said: Should a leather bottle have a hole in it as small as a needle's eye, all its air will escape. Yet, though man is formed with many cavities and many orifices, his breath does not escape through them. *(Genesis Rabbah 1:3)*

Notable Quotations

1. Be gracious to me, O God,
   For unto you I cry all through the day. (86:3)

2. I will thank You, O God, with my complete heart,
   And I will glorify Your name forever. (86:12)

3. There is none like unto You among the gods, O Lord,
And there are no works like Yours. (86:8)

Psalm 87

Theme: This brief psalm praises Zion as the center of the universal kingdom of God.

Outline: 1-3 Zion is city of God
4-6 Zion is the center of God's kingdom
7 Universal rejoicing

Liturgical Use: None

Practical Use: When visiting the Holy Land.

Legends: This tale is a commentary on the verse "As well the singers as the players on instruments shall be there: all my Springs are in You" *[Psalm 87:7].*

"As well as the singers as the players on instruments shall be there: All my springs are in You" *[Psalm 87:7].* Rabbi Yuda said in the name of Rabbi Meir: Like the spring form which fresh water pours out at every moment, so will the children of Israel sing a new song at every moment.

But the sages expounded: Even as the men will sing songs, so also will the women, as is said, "All my springs are in You." Here the word "springs" implies women, as in the verse "A garden shut up is my sister, my bride, a fountain sealed, a spring shut up" *[Song of Songs 4:12]. (Midrash Tehillim 87:7)*

Notable Quotations

1. God loves the gates of Zion
   More than all the dwellings of Jacob. (87:2)

2. Whether they sing or dance,
   All my thoughts are in you. (87:7)

Psalm 88

Theme: A lament of a person afflicted with a mortal illness and much suffering. Some have called this psalm the saddest of them all.

Outline: 1-8 Cry for mercy
9-12 Importunity of prayer
13-18 Psalmist will continue to rely on God

Liturgical Use: None

Practical Use: i. Feeling abandoned
ii. When experiencing great troubles and distress

Legends: This tale comments on the verse "The dead cannot praise God." [*Psalm 115:17]*

"The dead cannot praise God." [*Psalm 115:17*] A man should always occupy himself with Torah and good deeds before he dies. Once he is dead, the obligation of Torah and good deeds ceases, and the Holy One gets no praise for him. Regarding this, Rabbi Yochanan cited the verse "Among the dead I am released" *[Psalm 88:6*] --when a man dies, he is released from the obligation of Torah and good deeds. (*Talmud Shabbat 30a)*

Notable Quotations

1. O Lord, God of my salvation,
   What time I cry in the night before You. (88:2)

2. I am counted with them that goes down to the pit,
   I have become a person that has no help. (88:5)

Psalm 89

Theme: A royal psalm in which the Israelite king prays for deliverance form his enemies.

Outline: 1-4 Lovingkindness and faithfulness of God
5-18 Hymn of praise
19-37 Divine promise to David
38-45 Contrast between divine promises and present reality
46-51 Plea for clemency
53 Closing doxology

Liturgical Use: None

Practical Use: Feeling anxious and in trouble.

Legends: This *midrash* enumerates three things that were given condition to the people of Israel.

Three things--the Land of Israel, the Temple and the dynasty of David--were given conditionally. Proof for the Land of Israel? "Take heed to yourselves, lest your heart be deceived, and the anger of God be kindled against you, and you perish quickly from off the good land" [*Deuteronomy 11:16-17]*. Proof for the Temple? "As for this house which you are building, if you will walk in My statutes..." [*I Kings 6:12*]; but if not, "this house which is so high shall become desolate" [*I Kings 9:8]*. Proof for the dynasty of David? "If your children keep My covenant...their children also forever shall sit on your throne" *[Psalm 132:12];* if not, " I will visit their transgression with the rod" [*Psalm 89:33]. (Mechilta, Yitro, Amalek, 4)*

Notable Quotations

1. I will sing of the mercies of God forever,

To all generations will I make known Your faithfulness with my mouth. (89:2)

2. O Lord, God of Hosts,
Who is a mighty one, like You, O God?
And Your faithfulness is round about You. (89:9)

3. Happy is the people that know the joyous shout,
They walk, O God, in the light of Your presence. (89:16)

4. How long, O God, will Your hide Yourself forever?
How long shall Your anger burn like fire? (89:47)

Psalm 90

Theme: Meditation on the shortness of human life and God's eternity. Called *The Psalm of Moses*, there is a clear similarity of its language and thought to Deuteronomy 33. Psalm 90 begins Book 4 of the Psalter.

Outline: 1-6 God is an everlasting refuge
7-12 Misery of a life spent under Divine displeasure
13-17 Prayer for restoration of Divine favor

Liturgical Use: Appears in the preliminary service in the prayerbook as one of the daily psalms to be recited. It is also one of the ten so-called healing psalms of Rabbi Nachman of Breslov.

Practical Use: Desire to repent

Legends: This tale explores the question of the place where God dwells.

Rabbi Isaac taught: A verse in Deuteronomy speaks of "the skies, the dwelling place of the eternal God' *[Deuteronomy 33:27*]. But we would not have known whether the Holy Blessed One is the dwelling place of the world or whether the world is the dwelling place of the Holy Blessed One, unless Moses had come and given us the answer by saying, "God, You have been our dwelling place in all generations." *[Psalm 90:1] (Genesis Rabbah 68:9)*

Notable Quotations

1. Before the mountains were created,
   Or You had formed the earth and the world,
   Even from everlasting to everlasting You are God. (90:2)

2. Teach us to number our days,

So that we may get a heart of wisdom. (90:12)

3. Satisfy us in the morning with Your kindness,
   That we may rejoice and be happy all our days. (90:14)

Psalm 91

Theme: A royal psalm of trust in God's security.

Outline: 1-2 God is a sure defense
3-8 God's providential care
9-16 Reassurance of divine protection

Liturgical Use: One of the psalms in the preliminary morning worship service, recited daily. This psalm is used popularly used at the cemetery because of its theme in trust in God.

Practical Use: When in need of God's help and protection.

Legends: This tale, in the name of Rabbi Meir, speaks of receiving an angel for each mitzvah that a person performs.

Rabbi Meir said: When a person performs one precept, he is given one angel; two precepts, he is given two angels; many precepts, he is given many angels, as is said, "For God will give His angels charge over you" *[Psalm 91:11].* Why? To protect the person from demons as is said, "A thousand shall fall at your side. *[Psalm 91:7] (Tanchuma, Vayetze, parag. 3)*

Notable Quotations

1. Dwelling in the shelter of the Most High,
   Abiding in the shadow of the Almighty.
   I will say of God, who is my refuge and fortress,
   My God, in whom I trust. (91:1-2)

2. You shall not fear the terror by night,
   Nor the arrow that flies by day. (91:5)

3. He shall call on Me and I will respond to him

I will be with him in time of trouble,
I will rescue him and bring him honor. (91:15)

Psalm 92

Theme: A royal psalm of thanksgiving. *Psalm 92* is known as the Sabbath hymn, where it was in ancient times chanted each Sabbath by the Levites in the Temple. The commentator Rashi states that Psalm 92 was chosen for the Sabbath because it speaks of a future world which is an unending Sabbath.

Outline: 1-3 Joy of praise and thanksgiving
4-8 God's works
9-15 Proof of God's supremacy and the triumph of righteous people

Liturgical Use: It was chanted by the Levites each Sabbath in the Temple and is recited at both the Friday *Kabbalat Shabbat* evening services and Saturday morning Sabbath worship services.

Practical Use: When feeling thankful.

Legends: This is a tale about Cain when he left the presence of God.

"Cain went out from the presence of God" *[Genesis 4:16].* How can it be said that a man went out from the presence of God?" However, according to Rabbi Yudan, citing Rabbi Aibu, the verse signifies that Cain left his consciousness of the Lord's Presence by tossing off the words ["My sin is greater than can be forgiven"], as if by mouthing them he could blunt the Almighty's awareness of his sin. (*Genesis Rabbah 22:12)*

Notable Quotations

1. It is good to give thanks to Adonai,
   And to praise God's holy name. (92:2)

2. Wicked people may grow as quickly as grass,
   But in the end, they will be destroyed forever. (92:8)

3. The good will bloom like a date-palm,
   They will grow strong like a cedar in Lebanon
   Planted in Adonai's house,
   They blossom in our God's courts
   They still bear fruit even in old age, still healthy and fresh. (92: 13-15)

Psalm 93

Theme: A hymn celebrating God's victory over the primordial forces of chaos.

Outline: 1-2 The Eternal Sovereign is God
3-4 The powers of earth threaten God's reign in vain
5 The testimony of God is sure

Liturgical Use: Recited on Friday evenings as the last psalm of the *Kabbalat Shabbat* service. It is also recited on Friday mornings during the daily morning service since *Psalm 93* was chosen as the Psalm for Friday.

Practical Use: When feeling thankful to God and realizing God's almighty powers.

Legends: This *midrash* is a commentary on the verse "The rivers have lifted up *dochyam*" *[Psalm 93:3*] using a variety of Hebrew wordplays.

"The rivers have lifted up *dochyam* [Psalm 93:3]. Rabbi Levi said: The waters were whispering to one another, asking "Where shall we go?" and answering, "To the sea ["*derech yam*]. To the sea." However, according to the sages, the waters said, "We are being crushed [*dakkim],* receive us. We are being reduced to submission [*medukakim]*, receive us." *(Genesis Rabbah 5:3; Midrash Tehillim 93:5; Yalkut Psalms, parag. 848.)*

Notable Quotations

1. God reigns, God is clothed in majesty.
   God is clothed, God has girded Himself with strength
   The world is established and cannot be moved. (93:1)

2. Above the voices of many waters,
The mighty breakers of the sea,
God on high is mighty. (93:4)

Psalm 94

Theme: A plea for divine judgment. Israel is greatly oppressed and prays that God's righteous judgments will be revealed to all her enemies.

Outline: 1-2 Supreme Judge invoked
3-7 Description of oppressor
8-11 Oppressor's belief refuted
12-15 Righteous will be vindicated
16-19 Security in God
20-23 Unjust rulers doomed

Liturgical Use: Chosen as the Psalm for Wednesday, the Levites used to chant Psalm 94 in the Temple on the fourth day of the week. (i.e., on Wednesday)

Practical Use: When feeling anxious or threatened.

Legends: Israel's three precious gifts is the subject of this *midrash*, taught in the name of Rabbi Simeon ben Yochai.

It is taught that Rabbi Simeon ben Yochai said: The Holy One gave Israel three precious gifts, each of them through suffering: Torah, the Land of Israel, and the world to come. The proof for Torah? "Happy is the man whom You chasten, O God, for thus You teach him Your Torah" *[Psalm 94:12].* The Land of Israel? "As a man chastens his son, so the Lord your God chastens you" [*Deuteronomy 8:5*], followed by: "The Lord your God bring you into the good Land" [*Deuteronomy 8:7*]. And the world to come? "The commandment is a lamp, and the teaching is light, and reproofs of suffering are the way to life to come" *[Proverbs 6:23]. (Talmud Berachot 5a)*

Notable Quotations

1. God, how long shall the wicked exalt?
   How long shall the wicked exalt? (94:3)

2. Happy is the person who You teach, O God,
   And instruct out of Your law. (94:12)

3. Who will rise up for me against the evil doers?
   Who will stand up for me against the workers of iniquity? (94:16)

Psalm 95

Theme: This psalm is an expression of joy in God's service. It, along with *Psalms 96-99* begin the *Kabbalat Shabbat* welcoming of the Sabbath service each Friday evening.

Outline: 1-2 Invocation to praise God
3-5 Greatness of God
6-7 Second call to worship
8-11 Warning against obstinacy

Liturgical Use: *Psalm 95* is the opening hymn of the Friday evening Sabbath *Kabbalat Shabbat* service.

Practical Use: When feeling thankful to God

Legends: This tale explains the verse "We are the people of His pasture, and the sheep of His hand" *[Psalm 95:7].*

"We are the people of His pasture, and the sheep of His hand" [*Psalm 95:7*] When are we His people? when we are the sheep of His pasture, as is said, "When you are My sheep, you are the sheep of My pasture" [*Ezekiel 34:31*]. But when we are lions, God hates us, as is said, "My heritage is unto Me as a lion in the forest. Therefore, have I hated her" [*Jeremiah 12:8]. (Midrash Tehillim 95:2)*

Notable Quotations

1. Come let us sing to Adonai with joy,
   Shout with joy for our Rock who saves us. (95:1)

2. Come let us bow down and bend the knee,
   Let us kneel before the Lord our Creator. (95:6)

3. For forty years I was wearied with that generation,
And said: It is a people that make mistakes in their heart,
And do not know My ways. (95:10)

Psalm 96

Theme: A song of praise to God, the righteous judge of all the earth.

Outline: 1-3 Call to universal praise
4-6 God's worthiness to be praised.
7-9 All peoples invited to worship God
10-13 All nature invited to acclaim God

Liturgical Use: Appears in every Friday evening *Kabbalat Shabbat* worship service, and immediately follows *Psalm 95.*

Practical Use: When feeling in a thankful mood and desirous of praising God.

Legends: This tale attempts to prove the fact that God created the world only for the sake of music and song.

The Holy One said: I will open the tongue of all flesh and blood, that they may sing praise before Me every day and proclaim Me King in the four corners of the world, because I would not have created my world but for the song and music that they intone for Me daily. And the proof that the Holy One created the world only for the sake of song and music? The verse "Glory and majesty are before Him, strength and beauty are in His sanctuary" *[Psalm 96:6]* "Glory and majesty before Him" in heaven, and "strength and beauty in His sanctuary" on earth. The precise meaning of these words is spelled out in "His glory covers the heavens, even as the earth is full of his praise" [*Habbakuk 3:3*]. And the proof that the Holy One created heaven to have it engage in song? The verse "The heavens declare the glory of God, and the firmament shows His handiwork" [*Psalm 19:1].* And the proof that ever since the Holy One created the earth, it hymns songs to God? The verse "From the uttermost parts of the earth have we heard songs. (*Alphabet of Rabbi Akiva)*

Notable Quotations

1. Sing a new song to Adonai
   Sing to Adonai, all people on earth. (96:1)

2. Tell all the nations of the world how wonderful God is,
   Tell them that Adonai is great, praised by all. (96:3)

3. Let the heavens rejoice and the earth be glad.
   Let the sea and all within it thunder. (96:11)

Psalm 97

Theme: God is the universal King and Judge of all the earth.

Outline: 1-3 God's manifestation as King
4-6 God's revelation
7-9 Effect upon idolaters and Israel
10-12 Israel's duty

Liturgical Use: Appears in Friday evening *Kabbalat Shabbat* service, immediately following Psalm 96.

Practical Use: When happy and feeling like singing

Legends: This tale is a commentary on the verse "Ashamed will be all those that serve graven images and boast of things of naught; bow down to Him, all you gods" ***[Psalm 97:7]***

"Ashamed will be all those that serve graven images and boast of things of naught; bow down to Him, all you gods." *[Psalm 97:7*] Rav Nachman said in the name of Rav Mana: The idol is destined to come spit in the face of those who worship it and put them to shame, then bow down before the Holy Blessed One--and cease to exist. (*Jerusalem Talmud Avodah Zarah 4:7; 44a)*

Notable Quotations

1. A fire goes before God,
And burns up God's adversaries round about Him. (97:3)

2. Zion heard and was happy,
And the daughters of Judah rejoiced,
Because of Your judgements, O God. (97:8)

3. God is saving up a special light for those who are good,

And happiness for the honest. (97:11)

Psalm 98

Theme: Call to nature to worship God and acclaim God Sovereign.

Outline: 1-3 Praise God for His mercy toward Israel
4-6 Let the whole earth worship God
7-9 Let all nature rejoice in the worship of the true God

Liturgical Use: Appears in the Friday evening *Kabbalat Shabbat* service, and immediately follows *Psalm 98.*

Practical Use: When experiencing a wondrous nature event, such as taking a walk in a forest and marveling over its beauty.

Legends: This is tale told in the name of Rabbi Abba concerning why the people of Bet Shemesh were smitten.

It is said in the name of Rabbi Abba: Why were the people of Bet Shemesh smitten? Because they behaved disrespectfully toward the Ark, so that the Holy One was constrained to say: If a hen belonging to one of the people of Bet Shemesh had been lost, would not its owner have gone around to many doorways to recover it? Yet My Ark has been seven months in the country of the Philistines, and not one of you gave it any heed. Since you are not giving it any heed, it is for Me to give heed to it. [God's bestirring Himself for the Ark is set forth in the verse] "His right hand and His holy arm has wrought deliverance for Him" *[Psalm 98:1]. (Genesis Rabbah 54:4)*

Notable Quotations

1. Sing a new song to Adonai, for God has done wonderful things. God's great power has won victory. (98:1)

2. With trumpets and shofar sound,

Play joyously before the Ruler: Adonai.
Let the sea and all within it thunder,
The world and all who live in it. (98:6-7)

3. Let the rivers applaud, the mountains sing joyously together before Adonai.

For God is coming to rule the earth. God will rule the world and all its people justly and fairly.
(98:8-9)

Psalm 99

Theme: A hymn in praise of God's sovereignty and God's holiness.

Outline: 1-3 God is enthroned
4-5 God's rule is just
6-9 Holiness of God's reign

Liturgical Use: Appears in Friday evening *Kabbalat Shabbat* service, immediately following *Psalm 98*. Verse 9 "Exalt the Lord our God, and worship at His holy mountain" is also customarily recited by the congregation (on the mornings when the Torah is read) when the Torah is taken from the Ark and carried around the synagogue sanctuary before it is read.

Practical Use: When feeling in a happy or thankful mood.

Legends: This tale comments on the verse "You have established harmony" (*Psalm 99:4)*

"You have established harmony" [*Psalm 99:4*] Rabbi Alexandri said: Two ass drivers who hated each other were walking on a road when the ass of one lay down under its burden. His companion saw it, and at first he passed on. But then he reflected: Is it not written in the Torah, "If you see the ass of him that hates you lying prostrate under its burden...you shall surely release it with him" [*Exodus 23:5]?* So, he returned, lent a hand, and helped his enemy in loading and unloading. He began talking to his enemy: "Release a bit here, pull up over there, unload over here." Thus, peace came about between them, so that the driver of the overloaded ass said, "Did I not suppose that he hated me? But look how compassionate he was with me." By and by, the two entered an inn, ate and drank together, and became fast friends. What caused them to make peace and become friends quickly? Because one of them kept what is written in the Torah, Hence, "You have established harmony."

(*Tanchuma Mishpatim, parag 1; Midrash Tehillim 99:3)*

Notable Quotations

1. God is great in Zion,
   And God is high above all the peoples. (99:2)

2. God spoke to them in the pillar of cloud,
   They kept God's testimonies and the law that He gave them. (99:7)

3. Exalt God and worship at His holy mountain,
   For the Lord our God is holy. (99:9)

Psalm 100

Theme: A call to God's service, it is asserted that *Psalm 100* was traditionally sung in bygone years at the entry into the Temple court.

Outline: 1-2 Serve God with thanksgiving and gladness
4-6 Know God and God's goodness

Liturgical Use: Is recited at daily services in the morning during the so-called preliminary service.

Practical Use: When feeling thankful to God. Especially appropriate for recitation on the civic holiday of Thanksgiving during the traditional meal.

Legends: This tale, in the form of a word game, speaks of the death of the five disciples of Jesus.

The sages taught: Jesus had five disciples: Mattai, Nakkai, Netzer, Bunni and Todah...When the last of the sages, Todah, was brought before the court, he asked the judges, "Shall Todah be put to death? Is it not written, 'A Psalm for *todah" [Psalm 101:1]* They replied, Yes, Todah is to be put to death, for it is written, "Whoso slaughters *todah* [sacrifice of thanksgiving] honors Me.'" *[Psalm 50:23] (Talmud Sanhedrin 43a)*

Notable Quotations

1. Serve God with gladness
   Come before God's presence with thanksgiving. (100:1)

2. Enter in God's gates with thanksgiving
   And into God's courts with praise
   Give thanks to God and bless God's name. (100:4)

Psalm 101

Theme: The vow of an ideal king. It is hypothesized that it was written at the commencement of King David's reign.

Outline: 1-4 Preparation for the coming of the guest
5-8 Cleansing of the royal household

Liturgical Use: None

Practical Use: i. Especially appropriate in countries which have kings, to be used at their coronations.
ii. When feeling thankful

Legends: This legend, using a verse in *Psalm 101* and a wordplay, is a teaching of Rabbi Hisda concerning a person who speaks slander.

Rabbi Hisda said in the name of Mar Ukba: When a man speaks slander, the Holy One says, "I and he cannot live together in the world." So the Bible says: "He who slanders his neighbor in secret...him I cannot endure" R*[Psalm 101:5],* read not *oto* ("him"), but *itto* ("with him") [I cannot live]." *(Talmud Sotah 5a)*

Notable Quotations

1. I will pay attention to the way of integrity,
When will You come to me?
I will walk within my house in the integrity of my heart. (101:2)

2. Morning by morning will I destroy all the wicked of the land,
To cut off all the workers of iniquity from the city of God. (101:8)

Psalm 102

Theme: An individual lament of the psalmist who is afflicted with illness. Rashi the commentator identifies the speaker with Israel.

Outline: 2-3 Introductory invocation
4-12 Desperate state of Psalmist
13-23 Zion will be restored
24-25 Psalmist renews his plaint

Liturgical Use: None

Practical Use: When afflicted with an illness.

Legends: This brief tale utilizes the verse "Your servants take pleasure in her stones and love her dust." [*Psalm 102:15]*

Rabbi Abba used to kiss the cliffs of Acco. Rabbi Hanina used to repair broken sections of the roads in the Land. Rabbi Hiyya ben Gamda used to roll himself in its dust, in keeping with "Your servants take pleasure in her stones and love her dust." *[Psalm 102:15] (Talmud Ketubot 112a)*

Notable Quotations

1. O God, hear my prayer,
   And let my cry reach you. (102:2)

2. My enemies taunt me all day,
   They that are made against me do curse by me. (102:9)

3. You will arise and have compassion upon Zion,
   For it is time to be gracious to her, for the appointed time is come. (102:14)

Psalm 103

Theme: This hymn of praise and thanksgiving thanks God for five blessings: forgiveness of sins, healing of sickness, rescue from the netherworld, admittance to a good afterlife and the eternal enjoyment of God's heavenly bliss.

Outline: 1-5 Call to praise God
6-18 Divine graciousness
19-22 God the universal Sovereign

Liturgical Use: None

Practical Use: When in a thankful mood.

Legends: This tale describes the five worlds of David and the songs he composed for each one of them.

King David dwelled in five worlds and composed a song for each of them. When he abode in his mother's womb, he uttered the song "Bless God, O my soul, and all within which I am, bless His holy Name" *[Psalm 1-3:1*]. When he came out into the air of the world and beheld the stars and the planets, he uttered a song, "Bless God, you his angels...Bless God, all you His hosts" *[Psalm 103:20-21].* When, as he suckled milk from his mother's breasts and beheld her nipples, he uttered a song, "Bless God, O my soul, and forget not all those weaned from their mother's milk" [*Psalm 103:102).* When he saw the downfall of the wicked, he uttered a song, "The sinners are consumed out of the earth, and the wicked are no more. Bless God, O my soul. Halleluyah" [*Psalm 104:35].* When he reflected on the day of death, he uttered a song, "Bless God, O my soul; O Lord my God, You are very great; You are clothed with glory and majesty. You hide Your face, they vanish; you withdraw their breath, they perish" [*Psalm 104:1* and *104:29]. (Talmud Berachot 10a)*

Notable Quotations

1. Bless God, O my soul,
   And all that is within me, bless God's holy name. (103:1)

2. God is full of compassion and gracious,
   Slow to anger and filled with mercy. (103:8)

3. As for man, his days are as grass,
   As a flower of the field, so he flourishes. (103:15)

Psalm 104

Theme: A hymn to God the Creator, who reveals Himself in nature in this psalm.

Outline: 1-4 God's majesty in His creation
5-9 Creation of earth
10-13 Creation of springs and rain
14-18 Creation of food
19-23 Creation of moon and sun
24-30 Reflection on God's works
31-35 Concluding prayer and vow

Liturgical Use: This psalm has been chosen for recitation on every *Rosh Hodesh*, every new Jewish month. In addition, its first two verses "Let all my being praise God who is clothed in splendor and majesty, wrapped in light as in a garment, unfolding the heavens like a curtain" are often used as a meditation before putting on the tallit, a prayer shawl.

Practical Use: i. When in a thankful mood
ii. When appreciating God's work in nature

Legends: This is a tale about the daughter of Caesar, and it uses the third verse in *Psalm 104* as its primary Bible text.

The daughter of Caesar once said to Rabbi Joshua ben Hananiah, "Since your God is a carpenter--for it is written, 'Who lays the beams of His upper chambers in the waters' *[Psalm 104:3]* --ask Him to make me a spool." He replied, "Very well." He prayed for mercy in her behalf, and she was smitten with leprosy, whereupon she was made to sit in the open square of Rome and given a spool. Such was the custom in Rome: whoever was smitten with leprosy was given a spool, made to sit in the open square, and provided with skeins to undo and wind on the spool, so that people seeing him would pray for his recovery. One day, as Rabbi Joshua was passing through the Forum of Rome, he saw Caesar's daughter seated, undoing skeins and winding their wool on a spool. he said, "Is the spool that my God has given you good enough for you?" She replied, "Tell your God to take back what He has given me." Rabbi Joshua: "Our God gives, but never takes back." (*Talmud Hullin 60a)*

Notable Quotations

1. Bless God, O my soul,
   O Lord my God, You are very great.
   You are clothed with glory and majesty. (104:1)

2. How great are Your works, O God,
   In wisdom You have fashioned all of them.
   The earth is full of Your creatures. (104:24)

3. I will sing to God as long as I live.
   I will sing praise to my God while I am still alive. (104:33)

4. Let sinners cease out of the earth,
   Let the wicked be no more,
   Bless God, O my soul, Halleluyah. (104:35)

Psalm 105

Theme: A hymn of thanksgiving for past acts of God.

Outline: 1-6 Summons to proclaim God's mighty works for His people
7-12 God's faithfulness
13-24 God's protecting care of the Patriarchs
25-36 Display of God's power in Egypt
37-45 From the exodus through the desert to Canaan

Liturgical Use: One of Rabbi Nachman of Breslov's ten psalms of healing.

Practical Use: i. When in need of healing
ii. When in a thankful mood

Legends: This short tale is a commentary on the verse "Touch not Mine anointed ones, and do My prophets no harm" ***(Psalm 105:15)***

Rabbi Judah said in the name of Rav: What is meant by "Touch not Mine anointed ones, and do My prophets no harm" [*Psalm 105:15]?* "Touch not Mine anointed ones"--children in school; and "do My prophets"--the students of the wise--"no harm." *(Talmud Shabbat 119b)*

Notable Quotations

1. Give thanks to God, call upon His name,
Make known God's doings among the peoples. (105:1)

2. He has remembered His covenant forever,
The word which He commanded to a thousand generations. (105:8)

3. He brought forth His people with joy,
Those He chose with singing. (105:43)

Psalm 106

Theme: A national confession of sins and a prayer for help.

Outline: 1-5 Call to praise God for his unfailing goodness
6 Confession of sin
7-12 Experience at the Red Sea
13-15 Murmuring for food
16-18 Jealousy of Moses and Aaron
19-23 Golden Calf
24-27 Cowardice on return of the spies
28-31 Participation in Moabite worship
32-33 Sin at Meribah
34-36 Continued disobedience after entering Canaan
47 Closing Prayer
48 Doxology

Liturgical Use: None

Practical Use: When in need of help.

Legends: This tale is an explanation of the verse "Happy are they who do charity at all times." ***[Psalm 106:3]***

"Happy are they who do charity at all times" *[Psalm 106:3*] But is it possible to always do charity? Our masters in Yavneh (some say, Rabbi Eliezer) expounded the words as applying to one who sustains his sons and daughters when they are small. Rabbi Samuel bar Nachmani applied these words to him who brings up an orphan boy or an orphan girl in his house and enables them to marry. *(Talmud Ketubot 50a)*

Notable Quotations

1. Give thanks to God for God is good,

His mercy endures eternally. (106:1)

2. Save us, O Lord our God,
And gather us from among the nations,
That we may give thanks to Your holy name,
That we may triumph in Your praise. (106:47)

3. Blessed be the Lord, the God of Israel,
From everlasting even to everlasting,
And let all the people say Amen. Halleluyah. (106:48)

Psalm 107

Theme: A hymn of national thanksgiving that begins the fifth and final book of the *Book of Psalms.*

Outline: 1-3 Summons to praise God from the redeemed slaves
2-9 God's care of lost travelers
10-16 God's care of captives
17-22 God heals those who are sick
23-32 God's care of sea voyagers
33-38 God's control of man's habitation
39-42 God defends His people against attackers

Liturgical Use: None

Practical Use: When experiencing great trouble and distress.

Legends: This is a tale about an unusual sighting of Rabbah bar Bar Hanah.

Rabbah bar Bar Hanah said further: I saw Ormuzd the son of Lilith running so fast on the parapet of Mahoza's wall that a rider galloping below on horseback could not keep up with him. Once, the people of Mahoza saddled for Ormuzd two she mules which stood on the two bridges of the Robnag; and he jumped from one she mule to the other, and back again from the other to the one, while holding in his hands two cups of wine, pouring from one to the other, and back again from the other to the one, and not a drop fell to the ground. He was able to do so even though it was the sort of day when "waves mounted up to heaven and plunged down to the depths" *[Psalm 107:26] (Talmud Baba Batra 73a-b)*

Notable Quotations

1. Let them give thanks to God for His mercy,
   And for His wonderful works to the children of men. (107:8)

2. God turns rivers in a wilderness,
   And water springs into a thirsty ground. (107:33)

3. Who is wise, let them observe these things,
   And let them consider God's mercies. (107:43)

Psalm 108

Theme: A prayer for help against Israel's enemies.

Outline: 1-5 Resolution of joyous thanksgiving followed by prayer
6-13 Prayer for help and expression of assurance

Liturgical Use: None

Practical Use: When feeling anxious or in danger

Legends: This *midrash* attempts to explain the meaning of "My heart is prepared, O God: I will sing, I will sing praises. (*Psalm 108:1)*

"My heart is prepared, O God, I will sing, I will sing praises. (*Psalm 108:1)* Elsewhere, it says, "And I set My face unto the Lord God, to seek by prayer and supplications." (*Daniel 9:3)* But is not prayer the same as supplications? The distinction between them is this. Righteous men first incline themselves to the Holy Blessed One, so that He will listen to their prayers. And so our Rabbis taught: A man must begin to pray only in a mood of humility, not in a mood of lightness, nor in a mood of banter, so that the Holy Blessed One will listen to his prayer. (*Midrash Tillim 108)*

Notable Quotations:

1. My heart is steadfast O God,
   I will sing, yea I will sing praises even with my glory. (108:2)

2. Have you not cast us off, O God
   And You do not go forth, O God, with our hosts. (108:12)

3. Through God we shall do heroically,
   For God is that will tread down our enemies. (108:14)

Psalm 109

Theme: A cry for help, this psalm tells of suffering under persistent persecution. Rashi, the medieval commentator identifies the narrator of the Psalm with the nation of Israel.

Outline: 1-5 Plea for help
6-20 Cursing

Liturgical Use: None

Practical Use: When in need of help.

Legends: This is a tale about the journey of a wicked man.

If you are aware of a wicked man about to set out on a journey, and you intend to go in the same direction, start out as many as three days earlier or as many as three days later because of him, so that you will not have to set out with him on the journey, for the angels of Satan will accompany him, as is said, "Set you a wicked man near him, and Satan will stand at his right hand" *[Psalm 109:6] (Tosafot to Avodah Zarah, 1:17)*

Notable Quotations

1. In return for my love they are my enemies,
   But I am all prayer. (109:4)

2. I am gone like the shadow when it lengthens,
   I am shaken off as the locust. (109:23)

3. I will give thanks to God with my mouth,
   I will praise God among the multitude. (109:30)

Psalm 110

Theme: A king's victory is the theme of *Psalm 110.* Modern Bible scholars have identified the king as Simon Maccabee who combined the kingship with the office of High Priest. The ancient rabbis explained the Psalm as relating to Abraham and his victory over Amraphel. (*Genesis 14)*

Outline: 1-3 God's assurance of victory
4 The king's priesthood
5-7 Scene of battle

Liturgical Use: None

Practical Use: When wanting to speak to God.

Legends: This *midrash* uses the verse "I was with you when you did offer yourself willingly" [*Psalm 110:3*] to weave a tale.

"I was with you when you did offer yourself willingly.*" [Psalm 110:3]* The verse is to be understood as the Holy One's saying, "I was with you when for My Name's sake you willingly consented to enter the open fire. 'In the day of your hosts'--the day you gathered to Me all those hosts of people who, following your trial in the open fire, became converted. 'In beauties, holiness'--out of the beauties of the eastern part of the world, I hallowed you; 'from the very creation ["womb"] of the world I sought you out. Let it be the dew of your childhood to you'". Abraham was afraid and said, "Perhaps I bear guilt all those years I seemingly worshipped idols." Hence the Holy One went on, "Let it be the dew of your childhood to you'--even as dew evaporates, so have your sins evaporated. Even as dew is a sign of blessing for the world, so are you a sign of blessing for the world." *(Genesis Rabbah 39:8; Yalkut, Psalms, parag. 869)*

Notable Quotations

1. God at your right hand
   Does crush kings in the day of His anger. (110:5)

2. He will judge among the nations,
   He fills it with dead bodies,
   He crushes the head over a wide land. (110:6)

Psalm 111

Theme: The glorification of God for God's acts of mercy toward Israel. This psalm is an alphabetical acrostic, with each half line beginning with a new letter of the Hebrew alphabet.

Outline: 1 Promise of praise
2-8 Grounds for praise
9-10 Recapitulation of God's Mercies to His people

Liturgical Use: None

Practical Use: When in a praiseworthy or thankful mood.

Legends: This tale concerns the choice of verse for the beginning of the Torah.

Rabbi Isaac said: The Torah should have started with no other verse than "This month shall be unto you" [*Exodus 12:22],* which is the first precept enjoined upon Israel. Why then does it begin with "In the beginning" [*Genesis 1:1]?* Because "he wished to declare to His people the power of His works, to be able to give them the heritage of the nations without causing protest." *[Psalm 111:6*]. For should the peoples of the world say to Israel: You are a people of robbers, for you conquered the lands of seven nations, Israel will be able to reply: The entire earth and the fullness thereof belong to the Holy One. God created it and gave it to whoever seemed right to Him. So when God chose, God gave it to you, and when God chose, God took it from you and gave it to us. (*Genesis Rabbah 1:2; Yalkut, Bo, parag. 187)*

Notable Quotations

1. God's work is glory and majesty,
   And God's righteousness endures forever. (Psalm 111:3)

2. The work of God's hands are truth and justice,
   All of God's precepts are sure. (111:7)

3. The fear of God is the beginning of wisdom,
   A good understanding has all of them that do thereafter,
   God's praise lasts forever. (111:10)

Psalm 112

Theme: In alphabetical acrostic form, this Psalm describes the righteous person and his life.

Outline: 1-3 Blessed is the God-fearing person
4-6 Reward of the righteous
7-10 Permanence of the righteous and destruction of the wicked.

Liturgical Use: Often recited by a wife for her husband on Friday evening before the commencement of the Sabbath meal. May also be used in eulogies at funerals to describe the goodness of the deceased.

Practical Use: Uplifted feeling

Legends: This tale is about Rabbi Hiyya bar Ammi's statement that "one who lives from the labor of his hands is greater than one who fears Heaven,"

Rabbi Hiyya bar Ammi said in the name of Ulla: He who lives from the labor of his hands is greater than he who fears Heaven. For of him who fears Heaven, it is written, "Happy is the man that fears God" *[Psalm 112:1*]. But of him who lives from the labor of his hands, it is written, "When you eat the labor of your hands, happy shall you be; and it shall be well with you" [*Psalm 128:2]*. "Happy shall you be" in this world; "and it shall be well with you" in the world-to-come. (*Talmud Berachot 8a)*

Notable Quotations

1. Happy is the man that fears God,
   That delights greatly in God's *mitzvot.* (112:1)

2. Wealth and riches are in his home,

And his merit shall last eternally. (112:3)

3. The wicked shall see and be perturbed.
   He shall gnash with his teeth, and melt away,
   The desire of the wicked shall be destroyed. (112:10)

Psalm 113

Theme: One of the so-called *Hallel Psalms of Praise* to God, *Psalm 113* is a call to praise God.

Outline: 1-3 Call to universal praise of God
4-6 God's majesty
7-9 God's care for the lowly

Liturgical Use: As part of the *Hallel* Service, this psalm is recited on the pilgrim festivals (*Sukkot, Passover and Shavuot*) and on *Rosh Hodesh*. (the New Moon)

Practical Use: When feeling happy and in a praising mood.

Legends: This tale is a commentary on the verse "From the rising of the sun unto the going down, God's name is praised. *[Psalm 113:3]*

"From the rising of the sun unto the going down, God's name is praised." *[Psalm 113:3]*. From the time the sun begins to rise until it set, the praise of the Holy One does not cease from its mouth. Thus, you find that when Joshua rose up in Gibeon and sought to silence the sun, he did not say, "Sun in Gibeon, stop," but "Sun in Gibeon, be still" [*Joshua 10:12*]. For as long as the sun moves, it praises the Holy One, and if it praises God thus, it has the strength to move. Once it grows silent, it stops. Therefore Joshua said to the sun, "Be still."

The sun answered, "Do you presume to tell me to be still?" Joshua answered: "Yes." The sun replied: "But if I grow still, who will sing the praise of the Holy One?" Joshua replied: "Be still, and I will hymn song, as is said, 'Then Joshua spoke to God'" [*Joshua 10:12]*. Here the word "then," as in "Then sang Moses" [*Exodus 15:1*], suggest song. (*Tanchuma, Acharei Mot, parag. 9; Yalkut, Joshua, parag. 22)*

Notable Quotations

1. May Adonai's name be blessed now and forever,
   From sunrise to sunset, Adonai's name is praised. (113:3)

2. God lifts up the poor from the dust,
   The needy from the trash heap,
   And seats them with the nobles of God's people. (113:7)

3. God makes the childless woman happy with her children.
   Halleluyah. (Psalm 113:9)

Psalm 114

Theme: God's deliverance of Israel from Egyptian servitude is the theme of *Psalm 114.*

Outline: 1-2 Israel's choice by God
3-4 Nature's apprehension at God's might
5-6 Nature questioned about the effects
7-8 Earth bidden to tremble at God's presence

Liturgical Use: Chanted as part of the *Hallel* service on the three pilgrimage festivals as well as *Rosh Hodesh.*

Practical Use: Grateful to God for God's protection from enemies

Legends: This is a tale about why God redeemed the Israelites from Egyptian bondage.

Israel was redeemed from Egypt because they did not change their names. They went down there as Reuben and Simeon and came back up as Reuben and Simeon. Reuben was not called Rufus, nor Judah Julianus, nor Joseph Justus, nor Benjamin Alexander. Also, because they did not change their language--they continued to speak the sacred tongue, for Scripture says, "When the house of Jacob went forth from a people of strange language" *[Psalm 114:1],* and Joseph also said, "it is my mouth that speaks unto you"[*Genesis 45:12]* -- speaks to you in the sacred tongue. *(Leviticus Rabbah 32:6; Song of Songs Rabbah 4:12, parag. 1; Midrash Tehillim 114:4)*

Notable Quotations

1. Judah became God's holy people; Israel became God's nation. The sea saw and turned back; Jordan fled. (114:2-3)

2. What is with you, sea, that you flee.

Jordan, that you turn back?
Mountains, that you jump like rams; hills, like lambs?
Quake, earth, before the Ruler, before the God of Jacob. (114:5-6)

Psalm 115

Theme: A national prayer for God's help and an urging to retain confidence in God.

Outline: 1-3 Appeal to God for assistance
4-8 Contrast between God and heathen idols
9-11 Trust in God
12-15 God's blessing assured
16-18 Earthly and heavenly spheres

Liturgical Use: Chanted as part of the *Hallel Psalms of Praise* to God on *Sukkot, Passover, Shavuot* and on *Rosh Hodesh.*

Practical Use: When feeling great trust and confidence in God.

Legends: This midrashic statement is based on the verse *in Psalm 115:16* that "The heavens are the heavens of God, and it is the earth that God has given to the children of men." *[Psalm 115:16)*

We have been taught that Rabbi Yose said: The Presence never came down below, and Moses and Elijah never ascended on high, for Scripture says, "The heavens are the heavens for God, and it is the earth that God has given to the children of men." *[Psalm 115:16] (Talmud Sukkah 5a)*

Notable Quotations

1. Not because we deserve it, Adonai, but for Your own reasons act gloriously,
   For the sake of Your lovingkindness and Your truth. (115: 1)

2. Their idols are just silver and gold, made by human hands.
   They have a mouth and can't speak, eyes but can't see. (115:4-5)

3. Israel, trust in Adonai, our help and shield.
   House of Aaron, trust in Adonai, our help and shield. (115: 9-10)

Psalm 116

Theme: A personal hymn of thanksgiving to God, in which the psalmist records his personal experience as testimony to God's saving grace and power.

Outline: 1-2 Answered prayer demands loving gratitude
3-4 Prayer in peril
5-6 Revelation of God's character
7-9 Self encouragement based on God's mercy
10-14 Triumph of faith and thanksgiving
15-19 God will offer His thanksgiving sacrifice

Liturgical Use: Recited during *Hallel* service on three pilgrimage festivals as well as on *Rosh Hodesh.*

Practical Use: When in a thankful mood.

Legends: This is the famous tale of four men who entered paradise and that which happened to each of them.

Our masters taught: Four men entered the Garden of Eden, namely Ben Azzai, Ben Zoma, Acher and Rabbi Akiva. Rabbi Akiva said to them: When you arrive at the slabs of pure transparent marble, do not say: Water, water. For it is said, "He that speaks falsehood shall not be established before My eyes" [*Psalm 101;7*]. Ben Azzai cast a look and died. Of him Scripture says, "Precious in the sight of God is the death of God's saint" [*Psalm 116:15*]. Ben Zoma looked and became demented. Of him Scripture says, "Have you found honey? Eat so much as is sufficient for you, lest you be filled therewith, and vomit it" [*Proverbs 25:15].* Aher mutilated the shoots. Rabbi Akiva departed unscathed. (*Talmud Hagigah 14b)*

Notable Quotations

1. How can I pay Adonai back for all God's gifts to me. (116:12)

2. I will publicly keep my promises to Adonai, in the courts of Adonai's House, In the center of Jerusalem, Halleluyah. (116:18-19)

Psalm 117

Theme: The shortest of the entire Book of Psalms, *Psalm 117* is a summons to all the nations of the world to offer praise to God.

Outline: 1-2 Praise God for His truth lasts forever.

Practical Use: Recited during *Hallel* Service on pilgrimage festivals as well as on *Rosh Hodesh.*

Legends: This tale is about the three men who were thrown into the fiery furnace by King Nebuchadnezzar.

Rabbi Simeon the Shilonite expounded: When the wicked Nebuchadnezzar cast Hananiah, Mishael, and Azariah into the fiery furnace, Yurkami, the heavenly prince of hail, appeared before the Holy One and said, "Master of the universe, let me go down, cool the furnace, and thus save those righteous men from the fiery furnace." Gabriel spoke up, "The might of the Holy One will not be made evident this way, for you are the prince of hail, and everyone knows that water quenches fire. But I am the prince of fire. Let me do down, and I shall cook it within and heat it without, and thus perform a miracle within a miracle." At that, the Holy One said to Gabriel, "Go down." It was then that Gabriel burst forth: "True is God forever" *[Psalm 117:2]*

Notable Quotations

Praise Adonai, all nations, praise God, all peoples.
God's kindness overwhelmed us. Adonai's truth is forever.
Halleluyah. (117:1-2)

Psalm 118

Theme: The last of the so-called *Hallel* Psalms of Praise, *Psalm 118* is a hymn of national thanksgiving to God. In has been asserted that it was recited as a thanksgiving hymn during the festival of *Sukkot* in 444 B.C.E.

Outline: 1-4 Call to praise
5-9 Israel acknowledges God as her deliverer
10-14 Victory through God
15-18 Grateful rejoicing
19-24 Entrance into the Temple courts
25-29 Vows, blessings and praises

Liturgical Use: Recited on three pilgrimage holidays during *Hallel* service as well as on *Rosh Hodesh.*

Practical Use: When in a thankful mood

Legends: This tale is prompted by Rabbi Jeremiah's question "What is the proof that even a Gentile who keeps the Torah is like a high priest?"

Rabbi Jeremiah used to say: What is the proof that even a Gentile who keeps the Torah is like a high priest? The verse "Which if a man does, he shall live by them." Scripture says, "This is the Torah of man, O Lord God" *[II Samuel 7:19]* --not "or priests, Levites or Israelites," but "of man." Scripture also says, "Open the gates, that the righteous Gentile may enter" *[Isaiah 26:2]* --not that "priests, Levites, or Israelites may come in," but that "the righteous Gentile who keeps the faith may come in." Scripture also says, "This is the gate of God; the righteous shall enter it" [*Psalm 118:20]* --not "priests, Levites, or Israelites shall enter it," but "the righteous shall enter it."

Scripture also says, "Rejoice in God, O you righteous [*Psalm*

33:1] --not "Rejoice, O you priests, Levites and Israelites," but "Rejoice O you righteous." Scripture also says, "Do Good, O God, unto the good" [*Psalm 125:4]* --not "to priests, Levites and Israelites," but "Do good unto God, unto the good."

Thus, even a Gentile who keeps the Torah is like a high priest. (*Talmud Baba Kamma 38a; Exodus Rabbah 19:4; Sifre Leviticus 86b)*

Notable Quotations

1. Out of my straits I called upon God.
   God answered me with great enlargement. (118:5)

2. It is better to take refuge in God
   Than to trust in man. (118:8)

3. Thank Adonai for being good, God's kindness lasts forever.
   Let Israel say: God's kindness lasts forever.
   Let the House of Aaron say: God's kindness lasts forever.
   Let those who respect Adonai say: God's kindness lasts forever.
(118:1-4)

Psalm 119

Theme: A declaration of joy which the Torah brings to those that conduct their lives using its ways. *Psalm 119* is the longest Psalm of the *Book of Psalms*, consisting of twenty-two stanzas to correspond with the number of letters in the Hebrew alphabet. Each stanza comprises eight verses all beginning with the same letter in turn until the alphabet is completed.

Outline: 1-8 *Aleph*: Beauty of loyal obedience to the Torah
9-16 *Bet:* Youth may be clean by loving God's law
17-24 *Gimel*: Torah learning gives a person strength
25-32 *Dalet:* Prayer for strength
33-40 *Hey:* Prayer that the psalmist may observe to do the law of God
41-48 *Vov*: Prayer that God will keep him strong
49-56 *Zayin*: God's law brings hope and joy
57-64 *Het*: Devotion to the law of God
65-72 *Tet:* Affliction can teach the right way
73-80 *Yod*: Psalmist prays that righteous may be comforted
81-88 *Kaf:* Psalmists will continue to stay faithful
89-96 *Lamed*: God's law cannot be shaken
97-104 *Mem*: Passionate devotion of singer to God
105-112 *Nun*: Law of God guides one's footsteps
113-120 *Samech*: Safety and inspiration in Psalmist's loyalty
121-128 *Ayin:* Psalmist's plea that God should deliver him because of his devotion to the law
129-136 *Pe*: Beauty and benefit of God's law
137-144 *Tzadee*: God's law is righteous and pure
145-152 *Kof*: Psalmist prays that he may be kept faithful to God's law
153-160 *Resh*: Psalmist prays for deliverance
161-168 *Shin*: Psalmist declares observance

and love for God's law
169-176 *Tav*: Determination to do God's law

Liturgical Use: Verses spelling a person's name in Hebrew are often used at funeral eulogy, an unveiling, or an event honoring a person.

Practical Use: When studying Torah

Legends: This *midrash a*nswers Rabbi Giddel's question: "What is the proof that one may swear to observe a precept?"

Rabbi Giddel said in the name of Rav: What is the proof that one may swear to observe a precept? From the verse "I have sworn and have confirmed it, to observe Your righteous ordinances" [*Psalm 119:106]*

But why? Has not a Jew been sworn to observe them ever since Sinai? True, but the verse shows that a man may by an oath stir his zeal to observe them. (*Talmud Nedarim 7b-8a)*

Notable Quotations

1. *Aleph* Verse: Happy are they that are upright in the way.
   Who walk in the law of God. (119:1)

2. *Bet* Verse: I have sought you with my whole heart,
   Let me not err from Your commandments. (119:10)

3. *Gimel* Verse: Open my eyes so I can behold,
   Wondrous things out of Your law. (119:18)

4. *Daled* verse: My soul melts away because of heaviness,
   Sustain me according to Your word. (119:28)

5. *Hey* Verse: Give me understanding so that I can keep Your law,

And observe it whole heartedly. (119:34)

6. *Vov* Verse: I will walk at ease
For I have sought Your precepts. (119:45)

7. *Zayin* Verse: Your laws have been my songs,
In the house of my pilgrimage. (119:54)

8. *Het* Verse: I moved quickly and did not delay
To observe Your commandments. (119:60)

9. *Tet* Verse: It is good for me that I have been afflicted,
In order that I might learn Your laws. (119:71)

10. *Yod* Verse: Let those who fear You return to me,
And they that know Your testimonies. (119:79)

11. *Kaf* Verse: My soul pines for Your salvation,
In Your word do I hope. (119:81)

12. *Lamed* Verse: Your faithfulness is unto all generations,
You have established the earth and it stands firm. (119:90)

13. *Mem* Verse: How I love Your law,
It is my mediation all day. (119:97)

14. *Nun* Verse: Your word is a lamp unto my feet,
And a light for my path. (119:105)

15. *Samech* Verse: Depart from me, evil doers,
That I may keep the mitzvot of God. (119:115)

16. *Ayin* Verse: I love Your commandments,
Even more than gold, even fine gold. (119:127)

17. *Pey* Verse: Make Your face to shine upon Your servant,
And teach me Your laws. (119:135)

18. *Tzadee* Verse: I am small and hated,
Yet I have not forgotten Your precepts. (119:141)

19. *Kuf* Verse: I rose early at dawn and cried,
I hoped in Your word. (119:147)

20. *Resh* Verse: Salvation is far from the wicked,
For they do not seek Your statutes. (119:155)

21. *Shin* Verse: I hate and despise falsehood,
I do love Your law. (119:163)

22. Tav Verse: Let my tongue sing of Your word,
For all Your mitzvot are righteousness. (119:172)

Psalm 120

Theme: *Psalm 120* is one of a group of the so-called fifteen *Songs of Ascents*, each bearing the Hebrew title *Shir Hama-alote.* Bible commentators have asserted that the songs get their names from the fifteen steps that led up from within the Temple to the Court of the Israelites. This psalm is a prayer for deliverance from slander.

Outline: 1-2 Prayer for deliverance
3-4 God punishes slanderers
5-7 Lament of an exile

Liturgical Use: Appears in the *Mincha* afternoon Sabbath service in many prayerbooks as a study psalm.

Practical Use: When in need of God's protection

Legends: This tale is based on the verse "What more can be given to you, what more can be done for protection against you, you deceitful tongue?" *[Psalm 120:3]*

Rabbi Yochanan said in the name of Rabbi Yose ben Zimra: What is meant by the verse "What more can be given to you, what more can be done for protection against you, you deceitful tongue?" *[Psalm 120:3]* The Holy One said to the tongue: All other parts of a man's body stand erect, but you lie prone. Most other parts of a man's body are outside; you are within. Not only that, but I encompassed you with two walls, one of bone (the teeth) and one of flesh (the cheeks). "What more can be given to you, and what more can be done for protection against you, you deceitful tongue?" (*Talmud Arachin 15b)*

Notable Quotations

1. O God, deliver me from lying lips,

From a deceitful tongue. (120:2)

2. All my thoughts are for peace,
   But when I speak, they are for war. (120:7)

Psalm 121

Theme: God is the protector and helper of His people.

Outline: 1-2 Help comes from God
3-4 The sleepless guardian
5-6 Divine protection
7-8 Promise of God's care

Liturgical Use: Often appearing in the *Mincha* Sabbath service, it is customary to study it during Sabbath afternoons.

Practical Use: In need of God's help and protection

Legends: This is a tale in the name of Rabbi Hanina that concerns the norm of the Holy Blessed One as compared to the norm of humans.

Rabbi Hanina said: Pause and consider that the norm of the Holy Blessed One, is not like the norm of flesh and blood. The norm of flesh and blood is for a king to sit inside while his servants guard him on the outside. But such is not the norm of the Holy Blessed One. His servants sit inside while He guards them from the outside, as is said, God is your keeper, God is your shade upon your right hand." *[Psalm 121:5] (Talmud Menachot 33b)*

Notable Quotations

1. I will lift up my eyes to the mountains,
   What is the source of my help. (121:1)

2. God is your keeper.
   God is our shade upon your right hand. (121:5)

3. God shall guard your going out and your coming in,

From this time forth and forevermore. (121:8)

Psalm 122

Theme: A pilgrim to the Temple and his joyous meditation after returning home from his visit.

Outline: 1 Invitation to join the pilgrimage
2-5 Impressions made by the sight of Jerusalem
6-9 Prayer for the welfare of Jerusalem

Liturgical Use: A Psalm for the afternoon Sabbath *Mincha* service.

Practical Use: In the synagogue

Legends: This is a tale about scorners living in the time of King David.

No generation is without its scorners. What did such impudent ones do in David's generation? They would go to David's windows and say: David, David, when will the Temple be built? When will we be able to go to the house of God? And David would say to himself: Although they intend to provoke me, may such and such befall me if I did not rejoice should what they ask be fulfilled. That David spoke thus is implied in the word "I rejoiced when they said to me: 'Would that we were able to go to the house of the Lord'" *[Psalm 122:1] (Jerusalem Talmud Berachot 2:1, 4b; Jerusalem Talmud Shekalim 2:7, 47a; Yalkut Psalms, parag. 879.)*

Notable Quotations

1. Our feet are standing within your gates, O Jerusalem,
   Jerusalem, you are built as a city
   That is compact together. (122:2-3)

2. Peace be within your walls,
   And prosperity within your palaces. (122:7)

3. For the sake of the house of the Lord our God
I will seek your good. (122:9)

Psalm 123

Theme: A hymn longing for God's presence at a time when one is in trouble and looking for relief.

Outline: 1-2 Hope in God

Liturgical Use: A psalm recited during the afternoon Sabbath *Mincha* service.

Practical Use: Need to increase one's trust in God.

Legends: This tale is a commentary on the verse "Your wife shall be as a fruitful vine and as the altar's sides in your house" [*Psalm 128:3]*

"Your wife shall be as a fruitful vine and as the altar's side in your house." [*Psalm 128:3]* Rabbi Pinchas the Priest bar Hama said: So long as a wife is retiring in demeanor in her house, then even as the altar procures forgiveness, so she procures forgiveness for her household. *(Talmud Megillah 14b)*

Notable Quotations

1. Be gracious unto us, O God, be gracious to us,
For we are filled with contempt. (123:3)

2. Our soul is filled with the scorning of those that are at complacent,
And with the contempt of the proud oppressors. (123:4)

Psalm 124

Theme: A hymn of thanksgiving for being rescued by enemies.

Outline: 1-5 The peril
6-8 Thanksgiving to God

Liturgical Use: Recited at the afternoon Sabbath *Mincha* service.

Practical Use: When feeling thankful after escaping a dangerous situation.

Legends: This tale is a commentary on the verse "Or has God assayed to go and take Him a nation from the midst of another nation." [*Deuteronomy 4:34]*

"Or has God assayed to go and take Him a nation from the midst of another nation?" *[Deuteronomy 4:34*] Rabbi Avin taught in the name of Rabbi Simon: What is meant by "from the midst of another nation?" That the children of Israel were swallowed up in the very innards of Egypt, as is said, "They had swallowed us up alive." *[Psalm 124:3] (Midrash Tehillim 114:6)*

Notable Quotations

1. Blessed be God,
   Who has not given us as a prey to their teeth. (124:6)

2. Our help is in the name of God
   Who made heaven and earth. (124:8)

Psalm 125

Theme: A supplication in the form of a group lament for deliverance from the enemy.

Outline: 1-2 Confidence in God
3-5 Protection for the faithful and destruction for apostates

Liturgical Use: At *Mincha* afternoon service on the Sabbath.

Practical Use: Need to increase trust in God.

Legends: This legend deals with Resh Lakish's expounding on the theme of the suspected adulterous wife.

Rabbi Samuel bar Isaac said: When Resh Lakish began to expound on the theme of a wife suspected of infidelity, he would say, "A man is paired with a woman in keeping with the kind of person he is. Thus it is said, 'The rod of wickedness shall not rest upon the lot of the righteous'" [*Psalm 125:3].* Rabbah bar Bar Hanah said in the name of Rabbi Yochanan: Pairing a man and a woman is as difficult as the splitting of the Red Sea, as is said, "When God brings single people to dwell together in marriage, He brought forth the imprisoned Israelites into prosperity" [*Psalm 68:7].* But is it so? Did not Rabbi Judah say in the name of Rav: Forty days before the formation of a child, a divine voice goes forth and proclaims, "The daughter of so-and-so is to be given to so-and-so, the house of so-and-so to so-and-so, the field of so-and-so to so-and-so?" There is no contradiction, however, for Rabbi Judah's statement refers to first marriage. The preceding two statements to a second marriage. (*Talmud Sotah 2a)*

Notable Quotations

1. As the mountains are round about Jerusalem,
   So God is round about His people.
   From this time and forever. (125:2)

2. Do, good, O God, to the good people,
   And to them that are upright in their hearts. (125:4)

Psalm 126

Theme: A hymn of thanksgiving for past help and a petition for prosperity.

Outline: 1-3 God has already done wondrous things
4 Prayer for completion of restoration
5-6 Expression of faith for final outcome

Liturgical Use: At the Sabbath afternoon *Mincha* service. Also used as the introductory paragraph to the Grace after the meal.

Practical Use: When in need of God's trust

Legends: This is a tale in the name of Rabbi Simeon ben Yochai about laughter.

Rabbi Yochanan said in the name of Rabbi Simeon ben Yochai: It is forbidden for a man to fill his mouth with laughter in this world, for Scripture says, "Then will our mouth be filled with laughter, and our tongue with singing" [*Psalm 126:2]* When? "When it will be said among the nations: 'God has done great things with these'"

It was told of Resh Lakish that, after he heard these words from his teacher Rabbi Yochanan, he never again filled his mouth with laughter in this world. (*Talmud Berachot 31a)*

Notable Quotations

1. When God brought back those that returned to Zion,
   We were like unto them a dream. (126:1)

2. They that sow in tears
   Shall reap in joy. (126:5)

3. Though he goes on his way crying that bears the measure of seed,
He will return home with joy bearing his sheaves. (126:6)

Psalm 127

Theme: Composed for a king, this wisdom psalm stresses the fact that without the blessing of the true God, all human endeavors are fruitless. Thus it expresses one's utter dependence on God and God's help.

Outline: 1-2 Man's work fruitless without God
3-5 The blessing of children

Liturgical Use: At the Sabbath afternoon *Mincha* service

Practical Use: Needing God's help.

Legends: This is a tale based on Resh Lakish's statement that the world endures only for the sake of the breath of schoolchildren.

Resh Lakish said in the name of Rabbi Judah the Patriarch: The world endures only for the sake of the breath of schoolchildren. Not even for the building of the Temple are children to be deprived of their study of Torah.

Resh Lakish said to Rabbi Judah the Patriarch: I have a tradition from my forebears (others say, from your forebears) that if there are no schoolchildren in a town, it is bound to be destroyed.

Rabbi Judah the Patriarch sent Rabbi Hiyya, Rabbi Ammi and Rabbi Assi to go through the small cities of the Land of Israel to set up teachers of Scripture and teachers of Mishnah in them. When they came to a place where they found neither teachers or Scripture nor teachers of Mishnah, they said, "Bring us the guardians of the city." When the city's bailiffs were brought, the sages said, "Are these the guardians of a city? They may well turn out to be its destroyers." They were asked, "Who, then, are the true guardians of a city?" They replied, "The teachers of Scripture and teachers of *Mishnah.* As Scripture says, 'Except the Lord guard the city, the watchman wakes but in vain'" *[Psalm 127:1]. (Talmud Shabbat 119b; Jerusalem Talmud Hagigah 1:7, 76c)*

Notable Quotations

1. Except the Lord build the house,
   They work in vain that build it,
   Except the Lord keep the city,
   The watchman wakes but in vain. (127:1)

2. Children are the gift of God,
   The fruit of the womb is a reward. (127:3)

Psalm 128

Theme: A wisdom psalm whose teaching is that the person who worships and obeys God is rewarded with prosperity.

Outline: 1-4 Domestic happiness is a reward of godliness
5-6 Prayers and hope for the welfare of the community

Liturgical Use: At the Sabbath afternoon *Mincha* service.

Practical Use: Need to increase trust in God.

Legends: This tale concerns the way of life that is usual for Torah study.

This is the way of life usual for Torah study: You will eat bread with nothing more than salt, drink water by measure, sleep on the bare ground, live a life of privation, yet still keep laboring in Torah. If you act thus, "you will be happy, and it shall be well with you" *[Psalm 128:2]* --"happy" in this world and "well with you" in the world to come (*Ethics of the Fathers 6:4)*

Notable Quotations

1. Happy are all the fear God,
That walk in God's ways. (128:1)

2. May God bless you out of Zion
And may you see the good of Jerusalem all the days of your life.
And may you see Your
children's children.
Peace be upon Israel. (128:5-6)

Psalm 129

Theme: A national lament. Israel has suffered affliction throughout her entire history but has not been totally destroyed because God was on her side. Thus, the current good fortunes of Israel's enemies will be brief.

Outline: 1-3 Israel's past afflictions and deliverances
4 God has broken chains of oppressor
5-8 Hope for the future

Liturgical Use: Afternoon *Mincha* Sabbath service.

Practical Use: Anxious about one's enemies.

Legends: This tale is a commentary on the verse "And Jacob came *shalem* (in peace).

"A Song of Ascents. Much have they afflicted me from my youth up, let Israel now say. *[Psalm 29:1].* Said the Holy Blessed One to him: 'Yet they prevailed against you?' They have indeed not prevailed against me; thus "And Jacob came *shalem* ("whole")"

Notable Quotations

1. Much have they afflicted me from my youth up.
   But they have not prevailed against me. (129:2)

2. God is righteous,
   God has cut asunder the cords of the wicked. (129:4)

Psalm 130

Theme: The sixth of the penitential psalms, it is an individual lament--an expression of remorse for sin and a plea for forgiveness.

Outline: 1-2 Penitent's cry
3-4 God is a forgiving God
5-6 He awaits God's deliverance
7-8 Exhortation to the people

Liturgical Use: At the Sabbath *Mincha* afternoon service. It is also one of the penitential psalms recited during the Tachanun Supplicatory prayers in the morning. It is also recited after the prayer Y*ishtabach* in the morning during the Ten Days of Repentance (between *Rosh Hashanah* and *Yom Kippur)*

Practical Use: After committing sin

Legends: Following is a tale which is a commentary on the verse "I am the rose of Sharon." (*Song of Songs 2:1*)

Rav Abba bar Kahana taught that the congregation of Israel said to the Holy One: I am she, I am the beloved, deep in the depths of trouble, but when the Holy One lifts me out of my troubles, I shall freshen like a rose with good deeds and shall sing a song to God, as is said, "A Song of Ascents. Out of the depths have I called You, O God." (*Psalm 130:1) (Song of Songs Rabbah 2:1, parag. 1 and parag. 3)*

Notable Quotations

1. God, hearken to my voice.
   Let your ears be attentive
   To the voice of my supplications. (130:2)

2. I wait for God, my soul does wait,
And in God's word I hope. (130:5)

Psalm 131

Theme: A psalm of trust in which the Psalmist confesses humility and will be satisfied with whatever lot God chooses for him.

Outline: 1-2 A haughty heart denied
3 Perfect peace

Liturgical Use: At the Sabbath afternoon *Mincha* service

Practical Use: When in a mood of extreme humility and trust in God.

Legends: This tale identifies the historical occasions upon which David expressed humility.

"Lord, my heart was not haughty" [*Psalm 131:1]* when Samuel anointed me king: "nor my eyes lofty" when I slew Goliath; "nor did I strut in high office" when God restored me to kingship; "or in tending to marvels beyond my scope" when I brought up the Ark. "Surely I disposed my person like a weaned child with his mother" [*Psalm 131:2*]--even as an infant is not ashamed to be uncovered before his mother, so I disposed my person before You; I felt no shame in abasing myself for the sake of Your glory. (*Numbers Rabbah 4:20)*

Notable Quotations

1. God, my heart is not haughty nor my eyes lofty.
Neither do I exercise myself in things too great, or in things too wonderful for me. (131:1)

2. O Israel, hope in God,
From this time forth and forevermore. (131:3)

Psalm 132

Theme: A royal psalm that may have been part of the liturgy for the feast when the Ark was carried in procession to Jerusalem.

Outline: 1-2 Prayer to remember the pains David took to establish the sanctuary
3-5 Contents of the oath sworn by David
6-7 The people's cooperation
8-10 Prayers in connection with sanctuary
11-18 God's response to prayer

Liturgical Use: At the Sabbath afternoon *Mincha* service.

Practical Use: In the synagogue

Legends: This brief tale is a commentary on the verse "Your priests are clothed with righteousness" *[Psalm 132:9)*

"Your priests are clothed with righteousness" *[Psalm 132:9]*. These are the righteous nations of the world, such as Emperor Antoninus and his companions, who in this world are as priests of the Holy One. (*Yalkut Isaiah, parag. 429)*

Notable Quotations

1. Surely I will not come into the tent of my house,
   Nor go up into the bed that is spread for me. (132:3)

2. Let Your priests be clothed with righteousness.
   And let Your righteous ones shout for joy. (132:9)

3. If Your children keep My covenant
   And My testimony that I shall teach them,
   Their children also forever shall sit upon your throne. (132:12)

Psalm 133

Theme: The excellence of brotherly unity is the theme of this psalm. Some commentators have asserted that the psalm alluded to the effect of unification produced on the pilgrims by their common act of worship.

Outline: 1 Brotherly unity
2-3 Blessings of brotherly love illustrated

Liturgical Use: At the Sabbath afternoon *Mincha* service

Practical Use: In a group setting when one feels especially close to the others in attendance.

Legends: The following tale is a commentary on the verse "It is like the precious oil coming down upon the beard..." ***[Psalm 133:2]***

"It is like the precious oil...coming down upon the beard, even Aaron's beard." [*Psalm 133:2]*. Our master's taught: Two drops of oil like pearls hung from Aaron's beard. It is further taught--so said Rav Papa--that when Aaron spoke, they did not fall off, but rolled up and nestled in the roots of his beard. (*Talmud Horayot 12a)*

Notable Quotations

1. Behold, how pleasant it is
For brothers to dwell together in unity. (133:1)

2. Like the dew of Hermon
That comes down upon the mountains of Zion,
For there God commanded the blessing
Even life forever. (133:3)

Psalm 134

Theme: A pilgrim's choir leaving the Temple for the night, exhorting the priests and Levites to offer praise to God.

Outline: 1-2 Call to praise God
3 The priestly blessing in response to the call.

Liturgical Use: At the Sabbath afternoon *Mincha* service

Practical Use: As a prayer-blessing.

Legends: This tale is a commentary on the text 'The Lord send forth your help from holiness," and support you out of Zion. ***[Psalm 20:2f)***

An exposition of the text 'The Lord send forth your help from holiness," and support you out of Zion [*Psalm 20:2f]* Rabbi Levi said: All the boons, blessings, and consolations that the Holy Blessed One will in the future bestow upon Israel will come only from Zion. Salvation will come from Zion; as it says, oh that salvation of Israel were come out of Zion *(Psalm 14:7).* Strength will come from Zion, as it says, The rod of your strength God will send out of Zion *(Psalm 110:2*). Blessing will come from Zion as it says, The Lord bless you out of Zion. *(Psalm 34:3) (Leviticus Rabbah 24:4)*

Notable Quotations

1. Bless God, all your servants of God,
   That stand in the house of God in the night seasons. (134:1)

3. May God bless you out of Zion,
   Even God that made heaven and earth. (134:3)

Psalm 135

Theme: A hymn composed for use in the Temple, it is a call to praise God and God's might in both nature and history.

Outline: 1-4 Call to praise God
5-7 God's might in nature
8-12 God's might in Israel's history

Liturgical Use: Appears in weekday morning preliminary service, which includes many psalms of praise to God.

Practical Use: i. When feeling thankful
ii. In the synagogue

Legends: This is a story about differing views of cloud vapors, as asserted by Rabbis Yochanan and Simeon ben Lakish.

Rabbi Yochanan and Rabbi Simeon ben Lakish differed: Cloud vapors, said Rabbi Yochanan, come only from above, for they are described as "clouds of heaven" [*Daniel 7:13]*. But Rabbi Simeon ben Lakish said that cloud vapors come only from below, for "God causes the vapors to ascend from the ends of the earth" *[Psalm 135:7]*. Rabbi Yochanan's view is that God's giving of the vapors is like a man's giving a cask of wine to his friend, container and all. Rabbi Simeon's view is that even as man says to his friend, "Lend me a measure of wheat," and his friend declares, "Bring your basket and measure it out for yourself," so the Holy One declares to the earth, "Bring Me your cloud vapor, and you will receive rain." (*Genesis Rabbah 13:11)*

Notable Quotations

1. Praise God, for God is good.
   Sing praises to God's name, for it is pleasant. (135:3)

2. O God, Your name lasts forever,
 Your memorial, O God, throughout all generations. (135:13)

3. The idols of the nations are silver and gold,
 The work of human hands.
 They have mouths but cannot speak,
 Eyes but cannot see. (135:15-16)

Psalm 136

Theme: Often called the *Great Hallel*, the Psalm is a hymn of praise to God. The refrain "For God's mercy endures forever" in each verse was sung by the Levites in Temple times and today is chanted by the congregation in response to the prayer leader.

Outline: 1-3 Invocation to thanksgiving
4-9 God the Creator
10-15 God the Deliverer from Egypt
16-22 In the wilderness
23-26 God helps Israel as well as all humanity

Liturgical Use: Appears in preliminary morning service.

Legends: This commentary is based on the verse "O give thanks to God, for it is the bounty..." ***[Psalm 136:1]***

Rabbi Hisda said: The verse "O give thanks to God, for it is the bounty..." [*Psalm 136:1]* means, "Give thanks to God who exacts a man's debt from the bounty given to him--an ox from a rich man, a lamb from a poor man, an egg from an orphan, a hen from a widow." *(Talmud Pesachim 118a)*

Notable Quotations

1. Give thanks to God, for God is good,
   God's mercy endures forever. (136:1)

2. To God that made great lights,
   For God's mercy endures forever. (136:7)

3. Who gives food to all flesh,
   For God's mercy endures forever. (136:25)

Psalm 137

Theme: In this lament the psalmist, recently returned from Babylon, prays for vengeance on Israel's enemies.

Outline: 1-3 Exiles' singing is silenced
4-6 Refusal to sing
7-9 Prayer for vengeance upon the enemy

Liturgical Use: Recited on *Tisha B'Av*, the Fast of the *Ninth of Av* which commemorates the destruction of the Jerusalem Temples. This is also one Rabbi Nachman of Breslov's ten healing psalms.

Practical Use: When in need of healing.

Legends: This is a tale based on the verse "By the rivers of Babylon, there we sat down and wept." ***[Psalm 137:1]***

By the rivers of Babylon, there we sat down, yea we wept" [*Psalm 137:1*] What made Israel sit down and weep by the rivers of Babylon? Rabbi Yochanan explained: It was the Euphrates, which slew more of the children of Israel than the wicked Nebuchadnezzar had slain. While the children of Israel were living in the land of Israel, they drank only rainwater, running water or spring water. But when they were exiled to Babylon, they had to drink the water of the Euphrates and many of them died. And so the exiles wept for the dead who had perished in the way and whom the Babylonians had not permitted to be buried and wept for the dead whom the Euphrates had slain. They had even more cause to weep. For the wicked Nebuchadnezzar was seated in a ship, he and all his nobles and officers, and they had with them all kinds of instruments with which to sing, as is said, "The Chaldeans, in the ships of their singing" *[Isaiah 43:14*]. At the same time all the members of the royal house of Judah, who had been put into iron chains, were walking naked along the edge of the river. The wicked

Nebuchadnezzar looked up and saw them. He said to his servants, "why are such as these walking with their heads held high and without burdens? Have you no burdens to load upon their necks?" Instantly the servants brought Torah scrolls, shaped them into sacks, filled them with sand, and loaded them on the shoulders of the members of the royal house of Judah until their heads were bent low. At that, the members of the royal house of Judah said of themselves, "To our very necks we are pursued' *[Lamentations 5:5].* And in that hour all Israel moaned loudly, until their cry came up to heaven. *(Peskita Rabbati, 31:4; Yalkut, Psalms, parag 883)*

Notable Quotations:

1. By the rivers of Babylon,
   There we sat down and cried,
   When we remembered Zion. (137:1)

2. How long shall we sing God's song
   In a foreign land? (137:4)

3. If I forget you, O Jerusalem,
   Let my right hand forget her cunning.
   Let my tongue cleave to the roof of my mouth, If I do not remember you,
   If I do not set Jerusalem
   Above my chiefest joy. (137:6)

Psalm 138

Theme: A thanksgiving hymn to God for the fulfillment of God's promises.

Outline: 1-3 God is thanked for His mercies
4-8 God will be worshipped by all kings
7-8 God will continue to deliver Israel

Liturgical Use: None

Practical Use: Great troubles and distress

Legends: This is a tale based on the verse "All the kings of the earth, O God, admitted they were wrong after they heard the words of Your mouth." [*Psalm 138:4]*

Ulla the elder expounder at the entrance to the patriarch's house: What is meant by the verse "All the kings of the earth, O God, admitted they were wrong after the heard the words of Your mouth" [*Psalm 138:4],* in which it is said, not, "The word of Your mouth," but "The words of Your mouth?" The verse means: When the Holy One said, "I am the Lord your God" [*Exodus 20:2*], and "You shall have no other gods before Me" [*Exodus 20:3],* the nations of the world observed, "He is demanding deference to His own glory." But when He said, "Honor your father and your mother" [*Exodus 20:12*], they recanted and admitted that the first words were not merely concerned with deference to Him. (*Talmud Kiddushin 31a)*

Notable Quotations

1. I will give thanks with my whole heart,
   In the presence of the mighty I will sing praises to You. (138:1)

2. You I walk in the midst of trouble you keep me alive,
   You stretch for Your hand against the anger of my enemies. (138:7)

Psalm 139

Theme: A psalm of innocence composed by a religious leader who was accused of idol worship.

Outline: 1-6 God's perfect knowledge of the Psalmist
13-18 God has ordered the Psalmist's entire life
19-24 God nor the Psalmist can endure wickedness

Liturgical Use: None

Practical Use: When feeling close to God

Legends: This tale is an interpretation of the verse "God searches all hearts and understands every thought before its birthing" [*I Chronicles 28:9)*

Haggai, citing Rabbi Isaac, said that the verse God searches all hearts and understands every thought before its birthing" *[I Chronicles 28:9]* means: Even before a thought is shaped in a man's heart, it is already manifest to Him. In the name of Rabbi Isaac, Rabbi Yudan said: Even before a creature is brought into being, his thought is already revealed to Him. On his own, Rabbi Yudan, citing "For there is not a word on my tongue, but lo, O God, You know it altogether" [*Psalm 139:4*] said: Even before a man's tongue articulates a word, "Lo, O God, You know it altogether." *(Genesis Rabbah 9:3; Yalkut, I Chronicles, parag. 1080).*

Notable Quotations

1. For there is not a word on my tongue,
   But lo, O God, you know it all. (139:4)

2. If I ascend to heaven, You are there.
   If I make by bed in the netherworld, You are there. (139:8)

3. Search me, O God, and know my heart,
Try me and know my thoughts. (139:23)

Psalm 140

Theme: A lament in which the psalmist prays for protection and deliverance from personal enemies.

Outline: 1-3 Prayer for protection against persecutors
4-5 Repetition of prayer for deliverance
6-8 God the faithful helper in time of need
9-11 May deserved retribution overtake the evildoers
12-13 Destiny of the righteous and wicked

Liturgical Use: None

Practical Use: When in need of protection and feeling anxiety from one's enemies.

Legends: The following brief *midrashic* commentary is based on the verse "You protect my head on the day of kissing" *[Psalm 140:8].*

"You protect my head on the day of kissing" *[Psalm 140:8]* --the day when the two worlds kiss each other, the day a man leaves this world and enters the world-to-come. *(Jerusalem Talmud Yevamot 15:2, 14d)*

Notable Quotations

1. Deliver me, O God, from the evil man,
   Preserve me from the violent man.

2. Adonai, God, the strength of my salvation,
   Who has screened my head in the day of battle. (140:8)

3. I know that God will maintain the cause of the poor,
   And the right of the needy. (140:13)

Psalm 141

Theme: A sufferer from his fellowmen's sinful actions offers a pray asking for God's assistance.

Outline: 1-4 Supplication for divine aid
6-7 Effect of the judgement on the wicked
8-10 Prayer renewed

Liturgical Use: None

Practical Use: When in need of God's assistance and help.

Legends: This tale is based on the verse "And Abraham drew near--*[Genesis 18:23]*

And Abraham drew near--*vayigash [Genesis 18:23*], namely in prayer. Offerings *(muktar*) alludes to the evening prayer, as is borne out by the text, "Let my prayer be set forth as incense *(ketoret*) before You, the lifting up of my hands as the evening sacrifice." *[Psalm 141:2]*

Notable Quotations

1. God, I have called upon You, make haste.
   Give ear to my voice when I call to You. (141:1)

2. Guard my mouth, O God,
   Keep watch at the door of my lips. (141:3)

3. Let the wicked fall into their own nets,
   While I pass by in safety. (141:10)

Psalm 142

Theme: The lament of an Israelite for help while on his deathbed.

Outline: 2-5 His complaint
6-8 His petition

Liturgical Use: None

Practical Use: In time of illness.

Legends: This tale relates to the three daily services instituted by Abraham, Isaac and Jacob, according to Rabbi Joshua ben Levi.

Rabbi Joshua ben Levi said: Our patriarchs instituted the three daily services. Abraham instituted the morning prayer, for it says, "And Abraham got up early in the morning to the place where he had stood before God [*Genesis 19:27];* now standing refers to prayer, as it says, "Then stood up Pinchas, and prayed [*Psalm 106:30].* Isaac instituted afternoon prayer, as it says, And Isaac went out to meditate in the field toward evening *[Genesis 24:63*]: meditation connotes prayer, as it says, I pour out my meditation before God. *[Psalm 142:3*]. Similarly, I will meditate and supplicate, and God has heard my voice. (*Genesis 55:18] (Genesis Rabbah. Vayetze, 68:9)*

Notable Quotations

1. I cry to God with my voice,
   With my voice I make supplication unto God. (142:2)

2. When my spirit faints within me,
   You know my path,
   In the way where I walk

Have they hidden a trap for me. (142:4)

3. Attend to my cry, for I am brought low,
   Deliver me from my persecutors,
   For they are too strong for me. (142:7)

Psalm 143

Theme: Thematically similar to *Psalm 142*, this is a call for God's help and mercy.

Outline: 1-2 Plea for mercy
3-4 Overcome by persecution
5-6 Recollection of God's mercies
7-8 May God answer his prayer
9-10 Plea for deliverance

Liturgical Use: None

Practical Use: In time of need

Legends: Following is a tale based on the verse "If a man steal an ox or a sheep. *(Exodus 21:37)*

Rabbi Judah said: Israel said to God: 'There are many commandments here: If a man steal an ox, or a sheep (*Exodus 21:37];* because we stole and ox and made a calf, we had to pay five oxen in its place--namely, our ancestors died in the desert, and four sheep for a lamb--these are the four kingdoms who reigned over us; and because we stole Joseph, we spend four hundred years as slaves in Egypt.' Why is it that five must be repaid for one ox, and only four for a lamb? For an ox he must pay five, because he led him forth publicly. It can be compared to two people brought in judgment before the tribunal, one for having sold the son of the prince, and the other for having thrown a stone at the prince's statue. He that threw the stone received five lashes, while he who sold his son had to pay four hundred dinars to his master. Hence it says, 'Five oxen for an ox.' David said, And enter not into judgement with Your servant. *[Psalm 143:2] (Exodus Rabbah, Mishpatim, 30:7)*

Notable Quotations

1. Enter not into judgement with Your servant,
   For in Your sight shall not man living be justified. (143:2)

2. I remember the days of old,
   I meditate on all Your doing.
   I contemplate on the work of Your hands. (143:5)

3. Answer me quickly, O God,
   My spirit is dying.
   Do not hide Your face from me,
   Lest I become like them that go down into the pit. (143:7)

Psalm 144

Theme: This is a psalm praising God for His loving protection and blessings resulting from that protection.

Outline: 1-2 Praise for military assistance
3-4 God's goodness and man's insignificance
5-8 Prayer of the manifestation of God's power
9-11 Promise of eternal gratitude
12-15 Prosperity of Israel under God's protection

Liturgical Use: The verses "God what is man that You take account of him, or the son of man that You make account of him. Man is like a breath, and his days are as a shadow that passes away" are often used as introductory verses to the *Yizko*r Memorial Prayer service.

Practical Use: Grateful to God for success and prosperity.

Legends: This tale is a commentary on the verse "We are strangers before You. Our days on the earth are as a shadow" [*I Chronicles 29:15]*

"We are strangers before You...Our days on the earth are as a shadow" [*I Chronicles 29:15*]. Would that it were as the shadow of a wall or of a tree. But it is as the shadow of a bird in flight, for Scripture also says, "As a shadow that passes away" *[Psalm 144:4]*. "And without hope" *[I Chronicles 29:15]* --no one can hope that he will not die, for all know and affirm with their mouth that they will die. (*Genesis Rabbah 96:2)*

Notable Quotations

1. God, what is man that You take account of him,
Or the son of man that You make account of him?
Man is like a breath,

His days are as a shadow that passes away. (144:3-4)

2. O God, I will sing a new song to You,
Upon a psaltery of ten strings will I sing praises to You. (144:9)

Psalm 145

Theme: A hymn of praise to God for God's wonderful goodness and power. *Psalm 145* is an alphabetical acrostic with the omission of the verse beginning with "nun." A Talmudic rabbi once declared that whoever recites *Psalm 145* three times daily will be assured of a place in the world to come. This is because it contains the verse "You open Your hand and satisfy every living thing with favor." (145:16)

Outline: 1-3 Chorus of praise
4-11 Character of God calling forth His praise
13-17 God desires to make known His works
18-21 God ready to hear and answer prayer

Liturgical Use: Recited twice during every morning service and once in the afternoon *Mincha* service.

Practical Use: When in a thankful mood.

Legends: This tale concerns a Judeo-Christian who was a bother to Rabbi Joshua ben Levi because of his biblical interpretations.

In the neighborhood of Rabbi Joshua ben Levi there lived a Judeo-Christian who annoyed him with his interpretation of verses in the Bible. One day Rabbi Joshua took a cock, placed it between the legs of his bed, and looked at it steadily, saying, "When the right moment (of the day or night, when a cure takes effect), arrives, I will curse him." But when that moment did arrive, Rabbi Joshua had dozed off. On waking, he said, "This shows that it is not proper to attempt such a thing, for 'His tender mercies are over all His works'" *[Psalm 145:9*] Hence, it is not good for the righteous to attempt to punish" [*Proverbs 17:26]. (Talmud Berachot 7a)*

Notable Quotations

1. Every day will I praise You,
   And sing praises to Your name forever and ever. (145:2)

2. Adonai is good to all,
   And merciful to everything God made. (145:9)

3. You open Your hand,
   And feed everything alive to its heart's content. (145:16)

Psalm 146

Theme: God as the true helper is the theme of *Psalm 146.* This is the first of the so-called five *Halleluyah* Psalms with which the Book of Psalms closes.

Outline: 1-2 Exhortation and promise to praise God
3-4 Warning against putting trust in man
5-10 From the helplessness of man to the power of God

Liturgical Use: Appears in the daily preliminary morning service.

Practical Use: Need to increase trust in God.

Legends: This tale is based on a commentary on the verse "God loves the righteous." [*Psalm 146:8]*

"God loves the righteous"[*Psalm 146:8*] Why does the Holy One love the righteous? Because their worth stems neither from inheritance nor from family. You find the priests constitute an ancestral house and Levites constitute an ancestral house, as is said, "O house of Aaron, bless God, O house of Levi, bless God." *(Psalm 135:19-20*) According, should a man wish to become a priest, he cannot. To become a Levite, he cannot. Why not? Because his father was not a priest or not a Levite. But should a man, even a Gentile, wish to be righteous, he can, because being righteous does not depend on an ancestral house. Therefore the psalm says, "You that fear God, bless God" [*Psalm 135:20*] --not, "You house of them that fear God," because they who fear God do not constitute an ancestral house. But they themselves come forth on their own and love the Holy One. Therefore, does the Holy One love them. (*Numbers Rabbah 8:2)*

Notable Quotations

1. I will praise God while I live,
   I will sing praises to my God while I am alive. (146:2)

2. Happy is the person whose help is the God of Jacob,
   Whose hope is in Adonai his God. (146:5)

3. God preserves the strangers.
   He upholds the fatherless and the widow.
   But the way of the wicked God makes crooked. (146:9)

Psalm 147

Theme: The themes of this psalm are the good of God to Israel, God's beneficent care for all nature, and God's moral government of the world.

Outline: 1-6 Praise of God as restorer of Israel and ruler of world
7-11 Praise of God as the beneficent God of creation
120-20 Praise of God as giver of peace and prosperity.

Liturgical Use: Appears in daily preliminary morning service.

Practical Use: Grateful to God for success and prosperity.

Legends: This is a tale about the necessary criteria for the rebuilding of the city of Jerusalem.

Rabbi Samuel bar Nachmani said: According to an aggadah transmitted through the generations, Jerusalem will not be rebuilt until all the exiles have been gathered. If someone says to you: All the exiles have been gathered, but Jerusalem is still not rebuilt, do not believe him, for Scripture says, "God will rebuild Jerusalem" [*Psalm 147:2]* and then "God will gather together the dispersed of Israel." *[Psalm 147:2] (Tanchuma B, Noah, parag. 17)*

Notable Quotations

1. It is good to sing praises to our God.
   For it is pleasant, and praise is comely. (147:1)

2. God heals the broken in heart,
   And binds their wounds. (147:3)

3. God takes pleasure in them that fear Him,
   In those that wait for God's mercy. (147:11)

Psalm 148

Theme: A universal hymn of praise, summons all of nature to join in praise of God.

Outline: 1-6 Praise from heaven
7-13 Praise from earth
14 Israel has special reason for praising God

Liturgical Use: Appears in daily preliminary morning service.

Practical Use: In nature.

Legends: This tale is an argument between Rabban Gamaliel and a pagan philosopher regarding materials used by God in the creation of the world.

A pagan philosopher argued with Rabban Gamaliel: "Your God is a great artist, but surely God found on hand suitable materials which were of help to him." "What are they?" asked Rabban Gamaliel. The philosopher replied, "*tohu, bohu*, darkness, water, wind and the depths." Rabban Gamaliel exclaimed, "May the breath of a man such as you be blasted out. Since the term 'creation' is used by Scripture for all of them, it is clear that God Himself brought them into being. Tohu and bohu: 'I make peace [perfection] and create evil [lack of perfection]' (*Isaiah 45:7);* darkness: 'I form the light and create darkness' [*Isaiah 45:7];* water: 'Praise God, you heavens of heavens, and you waters' [*Psalm 148:4].* Why the water's praise? 'Because God commanded, and they were created' [*Palm 148:5*]; wind: 'For lo, God that forms the mountains and created the wind' [*Amos 4:13];* the depths: 'Where there were no depths, I created them'" *[Proverbs 8:24]. (Genesis Rabbah 1:9)*

Notable Quotations

1. Praise God from the heavens,
   Praise God in the heights. (148:1)

2. Fire and hail, snow and vapor,
   Stormy wind, fulfilling God's word. (148:8)

3. Let them praise the name of God,
   God God's name alone is exalted,
   God's glory is above the earth and heaven. (148:13)

Psalm 149

Theme: A hymn of triumph to celebrate a victory.

Outline: 1-4 Israel's praise due to God
5-9 Israel's enemies to be destroyed

Liturgical Use: Appears in daily morning preliminary service.

Practical Use: When in a thankful mood

Legends: This tale is a commentary on the verses in the *Book of Esther* "Then were the scribes called...and there was written...and letters were sent" [*Esther 3:12-13]*

"Then were the king's scribes called, and there was written, and letters were sent" *[Esther 3:12-13].* What was written in those letters? To all peoples of diverse races and languages: May your well-being increase. Be it known unto you that there came to us a man, who is not of our city or of our land, an Amalekite, the son of distinguished forebears, and his name is Haman. He put a small, one may say, trifling request to us, saying: In our midst there dwells a nation more despicable than any other nation. Arrogant in spirit, they are ever ready for treachery and corruption. They hold us in contempt and rejoice in our misfortune. Evening, morning and noon the cursing of the king is habitual in their mouths. They keep saying, "The Lord is king forever and ever. May the nations vanish from His earth" [*Psalm 10:16*] when "He wreaks vengeance upon the nations, punishment upon the peoples" [*Psalm 149:7] (Aggadat Esther, ed. Buber, p. 38)*

Notable Quotations

1. Sing to God a new song,
   And God's praise in the assembly of the righteous. (149:1)

2. God takes pleasure in his people.
   God adorns the humble with salvation. (149:4)

Psalm 150

Theme: Every living being is invited to praise God with every musical instrument.

Outline: 1-6 Praising God with musical instruments and with all of one's breath.

Liturgical Use: Appears in daily morning preliminary service. It is also one of Rabbi Nachman of Breslov's ten healing psalms.

Practical Use: i When feeling especially thankful
ii. Upon recovering from an illness

Legends: This is a famous saying in the name of Rabbi Jeremiah ben Eleazar.

Rabbi Jeremiah ben Eleazar said: Ever since the Temple was destroyed, it is enough for the world to use only two letters [of the tetragrammaton], *yod* and *hey*, as is said: "Let everything that has breath praise by saying *Yah*" [*Psalm 150:6] (Talmud Eruvin 18b)*

Notable Quotations

1. Praise God with the sound of the shofar,
Praise God with harp and lyre. (150:3)

2. Praise God with loud cymbals,
Praise God with clashing cymbals.
Let everything that breathes praise God. Halleluyah. (150:5-6)

Healing Psalms

In Jewish tradition God is often viewed as a source of healing. In fact, one of God's names is *HaRofeh—The Healer*. The Hasidic Rabbi Nachman of Breslov identified ten psalms has having special power to bring both healing of body and spirit. He designed them as the *Tikkun HaKlali, the Complete Remedy.* In his view, the ultimate goal is to bring the world into a state of *tikkun*—repair, wholeness and perfection. Prayer is integral to bringing about repair of the world. The sages taught that the *Book of Psalms* is built upon ten basic kinds of praise and song:

Rabbi Yeshshua ben Levi said: Through ten expressions of praise the *Book of Psalms* was composed. *Nitzuah, Niggun, Maskil, Mizmor, Shir,Ashrei,Tehillah, Tefillah,Hoda'ah* and *Halleluyah*. Greatest of them is *Halleluyah*, which contains praise and the name of God in one word. (*Talmud Pesachim 117a; Zohar III, 101a)*

The following are the ten Psalms that Rabbi Nachman identified as psalms of healing. The commentary is based on the description of each of the psalms by Rabbi Simkha Y. Weinstraub, program consultant of the Jewish Healing Center which offers healing prayer services, spiritual support groups and pastoral counseling to those who are ill as well as rabbis, chaplains and health care professionals.

Psalm 16: This Psalm starts with a powerful expression of trust and faith in God and gratitude for God's goodness. The Psalmist feels the nearness of the Divine Presence and confidence in Divine protection.

Psalm 32: This Psalm urges us to look deep into ourselves, to examine where and how we have distanced ourselves from God, and to return to God as the Source of true life and joy.

Psalm 41: This Psalm speaks explicitly about sickness, vividly portraying the torment and suffering endured by so many, expressing thanks to God for the possibility of healing, and stressing the need for caregivers to be sensitive, understanding and supportive.

Psalm 42: This Psalm depicts the yearning for God "as a hart thirsts for springs of water," describing the pain and suffering of both the individual and the nation in exile while affirming the hope of ultimate deliverance.

Psalm 59: This Psalm is a cry from the heart for God to deliver us from the forces that oppress us and cast us down, echoing David's plea for rescue from Saul's soldiers and his thanksgiving upon receiving Divine refuge and support.

Psalm 77: This is an important turning point in this collection, beginning with an expression of anguish and abandonment, the pain and persecution of a long, bitter exile—but moving into an affirmation of faith that God is ever-present and compassionate, despite appearance to the contrary.

Psalm 90: The Psalm offers a profound comment on human destiny, contrasting human frailty and the brevity of human life with God's eternity and omnipotence, asking God for wisdom, joy, security, support and compassion.

Psalm 105: This Psalm, after calls to sing and praise, traces the national history of the Jewish People from the covenant with the Patriarchs and Matriarchs through the Exodus from Egypt, which serves as a prototype of Redemption.

Psalm 137: This Psalm takes us back to the acute pain of exile, weaving in nine verses a tapestry of grief, despair, memory, affirmation, and anger…which may be viewed as the proverbial darkness that comes before the light, as these Ten Psalms conclude with *Psalm 150,* a paen and musical symphony of praises.

Psalm 150: This Psalm, the musical psalm with a mentioning of many of the instruments that were played at services during Temple times, is a challenge to praise God in the midst of illness. The last line of the Psalm of Rabbi Nachman's *tikkun (*repair of the world) brings an awareness of the breath. The last word of the Psalm is *halleluyah,* praise God. *Yah* is the breathiest name for God who breathed the breath of life into Adam and Eve, and each one of us.

Jewish Spiritual Practices and the *Book of Psalms*

Reciting *Psalms* is a traditional practice among pious Jews as well as people of other faiths. Many people know quite a number of the Psalms by heart, which they can recite while engaging in work or other daily activities. Some people carry with them a small *Book of Psalms*, and at any free moment when in need of a particular *Psalm* for a special occasion take it out and recite a psalm or two. Following is a listing of some basic Jewish spiritual practices and advice related to using psalms in one's life.

1.Recite psalms every day, and if you can complete the whole book every week, how good. (Rabbi Yechiel Michal of Zlotchov's *Hanhagot, #3, Zichron l'Rishonim, pg. 81)*

2. Study the *Book of Psalms* a number of times, so that the words and their translation will be thoroughly familiar to you, as well as Rashi's interpretation. Then you will well understand what you are saying when you recite *Psalms*. (*Tzvaat* Rabbi Yaakov mi-Lisa, #4, *YHvT, p. 68)*

3.You should find yourself and everything that happens to you in the psalms that you say. And all the thanksgiving in the *Psalms* you should say about yourself, for the kindnesses that God has done with you all your life. (*The Bratzlaver Seder haYom, #14)*

4.The *Psalms* were made for all the people of Israel in general and for each one in particular. The wars that every person has with his evil inclination and everything that takes place in his life, are all present in the Psalms and are explained there. Indeed, the whole *Book of Psalms* was said and established only with regard to the war with the evil inclination and its minions, which are the chief enemies and adversaries of man. (*Likkutei Aytzot ha-Meshulash, vol. 5, Tefillah, #15)*

5. Rabbi Nachman of Bratslav said: Whoever wants to merit becoming worthy of doing *teshuvah* (repentance), should accustom himself to saying psalms, for the psalms have a special power to inspire repentance, (*Likkutei Aytzot, Teshuvah, #32)*

6. Psalms can be used as a way to make supplication for God's help. When you are in need or in trouble, along with making your request to God in prayer, consider reciting Psalms as an offering and as another form of prayer to arouse God's mercy.

7. If a person has a need and a request to make to God, he should say Psalms with *kavannah* (proper intention) and with all his heart, and God, Blessed be the One, will help him. (*Maasiyot u'Maamarim Yekarim, p.25)*

8. The saying of Psalms is a *tikkun* (a means of spiritual repair) for sin. (*Or ha-Ner,* note on #7)

9. With regard to a number of a person's needs, such as his livelihood, or to various difficulties that a person might be in, Rabbi Pinchas of Koretz would instruct him to say the whole *Book of Psalms*, from beginning to end, without a break. (*Midrash Pinchas, pg. 13, #28)*

10. Some people use the unbroken recital of the whole *Book of Psalms* on the eve of the Sabbath to prepare for the Sabbath. Some say the whole *Book of Psalms* without interruption on *Shabbat itself*, either in the morning or in the evening.(Yizchak Buxbaum)

11. When you have committed a sin in your speech, repent by staying up all Thursday night learning Torah. Or if it is impossible for you to stay up the whole night, then, on the holy Sabbath, recite the whole *Book of Psalms* through without interruption. (Rabbi Mordecai of Tchernobil, *Hanhagot Tzaddikim, pg. 68, #19)*

12. It is better to get used to saying two or three psalms with intense *kavannah* (intention) than to be one of those who says all the psalms, quickly and without intention. (*Tzavaat Rabbeinu Yonah, #3,* in *Tzavaot v'Derech Tovim)*

13. If you are in a depressed mood, say psalms that will clarify the mood, such as 3,6,10,13,16,17,22,25,31,38,42, and especially 51, which you should say frequently. Or, if it is a happy mood, says psalms that increase the feeling of happiness, such as 1,8,9,19,23,24,27,29,30,33,34, and others songs and praises of God. (Rabbi Kalonymous Kalmish of Peasetzna)

14. There is a traditional prayer that can be said before one recites a few psalms:

May it be Your will, O God and God of our fathers, and mothers, to turn with compassion to hear these Psalms that I will recite, as if it were King David himself, peace be with him who is saying them. And may the merit of these psalms serve to atone for our sins and transgressions and wrongdoing, and to cut off the forces of negation and evil, to chop down the briars and thorns that surround the beautiful Rose on High, the Shechinah, and join the Wife of Youth, the Congregation of Israel, with her Lover, in love and affection. And may the recitation of these psalms bring down from on High a flow of spirit into our souls to purify us from our sings, so that our transgressions be forgiven and our wrongdoing atoned for; as You forgave David, who said these psalms before You, as it is written, "So God has removed your sins, you shall not die." (*Peasetzna Rebbe)*

Psalms classified for Reading and Meditation

Following is a summary of psalms classified for reading and meditation that appear in the Soncino Press Edition of the Book of Psalms. This summary will again assist you in utilizing these psalms for your own particular use:

The Godly life: 1, 15, 24, 26, 34, 101, 111, 112, 131

God's Revelation: 19, 119.

Meditation of Human Life: 49, 40, 139.

Penitential: 6, 25, 32, 37, 51, 102, 130, 143.

Problem of Good and Evil: 37, 73.

Righteous and the Wicked: 9-14, 27, 36, 44, 52, 53, 58, 59, 64, 94, 109

God and Nature: 8, 19, 29, 45, 104

God in History 68, 71, 81, 105, 106, 114, 136

Kingship of God 47, 93, 95-100

Yearning for God: 42, 43, 63, 84
God's judgment 50, 58, 75, 82, 83

God a sure Refuge: 7, 17, 18, 27, 31, 62, 71, 91, 121, 142

God the Deliverer: 46, 54-57, 74, 77, 79, 80, 85, 107, 116, 140,

141, 144,

Submission to God: 2, 7, 20, 26, 30, 32, 42, 52, 63, 67, 77, 84, 128, 141, 142.

Confidence in God: 3, 4, 9, 11, 13, 14, 16, 21, 23, 27, 34, 36, 37, 40, 41, 44, 46, 53, 56, 62, 65, 73, 91, 94, 108, 121, 123, 124, 125, 127.

Prayer in Trouble: 5, 6, 10, 12, 13, 17, 22, 25, 28, 31, 35, 38, 39, 43, 51, 54, 55, 57, 59, 64, 69, 70, 71, 74, 86, 88, 102, 130, 140, 143.

Praise of God: 8, 18, 24, 29, 33, 34, 47, 48, 66, 68, 89, 92, 93, 95-100, 103, 104, 107, 111, 113-118, 135, 136, 138, 145-150.

For Further Reading

The Book of Psalms: A New Translation According to the Traditional Hebrew Text. Philadelphia: Jewish Publication Society of America, 1972.

Cohen, A. commentary. *The Psalms*. London: Soncino Press, 1962.

Dahood, Mitchell. *The Anchor Bible: Psalms I, Psalms II and Psalms III.* New York: Double Day. 1965, 1966, 1970.

Glazer, Miryam. *Psalms of the Liturgy*. New York: Aviv Press, 2008.

Hirsch, Samson Raphael. *The Psalms. Translation and commentary by Rabbi Samson Raphael Hirsch*. Jerusalem and New York: Feldheim Publishers, 1978.

Mitchell, Stephen. *A Book of Psalms: Selected and Adapted from the Hebrew*. New York: HarperCollins, 1993.

Rosenberg, A.J. *The Book of Psalms: A New English Translation. Translation of text, Rashi and commentary* by A.J. Rosenberg. 3 vols. New York: The Judaica Press, 1991.

Weintraub, Simkha Y., editor. *Healing of Soul, Healing of Body*. Woodstock, Jewish Lights Publishing, 1994.

About This Imprint

The L'Chayim Library is a dedicated imprint of Higher Ground Books & Media focused on publishing works that explore Jewish faith, tradition, scholarship, and spiritual life. Guided by a commitment to accuracy, thoughtful reflection, and meaningful dialogue, the imprint highlights voices that contribute to the understanding and appreciation of Jewish heritage. Faith Advisor Rabbi Ron Isaacs serves as a subject matter expert for the imprint, helping ensure that titles reflect integrity and authenticity within Jewish thought and practice.

Other titles from L'Chayim Library

Haggadah Ask a Question by Ron Isaacs

HIGHER GROUND
BOOKS & MEDIA

Need Bulk Copies?

If you would like to order bulk copies of this book or any other title at Higher Ground Books & Media, please contact us at highergroundbooksandmedia@gmail.com.

We offer discounts for purchases of 20 or more copies. Excellent for small groups, book clubs, classrooms, etc.

Get in touch today and get a set of great stories for your students or group members.

www.ingramcontent.com/pod-product-compliance
Lightning Source LLC
LaVergne TN
LVHW020702110826
845149LV00012B/2069

9781971959016